Literature in Perspective

James Joyce

Kenneth Grose

Evans Brothers Limited London

Literature in Perspective
General Editor: Kenneth Grose

Evans Brothers Limited, London
Published by Evans Brothers Limited
Montague House, Russell Square, London, W.C.1

First published 1975

Set in 11 on 12 point Bembo and printed in Great Britain by
The Garden City Press Limited, Letchworth, Hertfordshire
SG6 1JS

cased ISBN 237 44815 7   PRA 4084

limp ISBN 237 44816 5

Literature in Perspective

Reading is a pleasure; reading great literature is a great pleasure, which can be enhanced by increased understanding, both of the actual words on the page and of the background to those words, supplied by a study of the author's life and circumstances. Criticism should try to foster understanding in both aspects.

Unfortunately for the intelligent layman and young reader alike, recent years have seen critics of literature (particularly academic ones) exploring slender ramifications of meaning, exposing successive levels of association and reference, and multiplying the types of ambiguity unto seventy times seven.

But a poet is 'a man speaking to men', and the critic should direct his efforts to explaining not only what the poet says, but also what sort of man the poet is. It is our belief that it is impossible to do the first without doing the second.

Literature in Perspective, therefore, aims at giving a straightforward account of literature and of writers—straightforward both in content and in language. Critical jargon is as far as possible avoided; any terms that must be used are explained simply; and the constant preoccupation of the authors of the series is to be lucid.

It is our hope that each book will be easily understood, that it will adequately describe its subject without pretentiousness so that the intelligent reader who wants to know about Donne or Keats or Shakespeare will find enough in it to bring him up to date on critical estimates.

Even those who are well read, we believe, can benefit from a lucid exposition of what they may have taken for granted, and perhaps—dare it be said?—not fully understood.

K. H. G.

James Joyce

The object of this book, as of all the other books in the Literature in Perspective Series, is to make a great writer's work intelligible to the ordinary non-scholarly reader. This object is perhaps harder to achieve in the case of James Joyce than with any other author: to understand Joyce, you would need to *be* Joyce, to exist in his mind and live in his circumstances, in his own space and time. This is of course true, in some degree, of any artist; but Joyce's work is intensely personal, a fact which holds considerable irony, since it was a main tenet of his aesthetic that the artist must always remain distanced from his creations.

The shape of this volume reflects the author's belief that most people will approach James Joyce through *A Portrait of the Artist as a Young Man*, but that *Ulysses* will always be regarded as the true embodiment of his genius. Hence half this book is occupied by a guided tour of *Ulysses*, with *A Portrait* as a prologue and *Finnegans Wake* as a brief excursion into an all but impenetrable jungle. Other works, such as the Poems, the collection of short stories, *Dubliners*, and the play *Exiles*, are treated as preparatory flexings of the muscles or as short cleansing flights undertaken as temporary distractions. Beyond these easily obtainable books this short introductory study does not attempt to go; the *Letters* and the *Critical Writings* are often fascinating, but are outside the limits of the writer's purpose.

Any student of Joyce must first of all give thanks for the great yet manageable biography of Richard Ellmann, of whose conversation on James Joyce and other authors I have been fortunate enough to have had the benefit. I must also thank my 1971 Division at Winchester, VICIa, for their stimulating comments on *Ulysses* and their refusal to let me get away with hazy critical statements. One of them, William Darling, now of King's College, Cambridge, found the passage in Plato's *Republic* which is printed on p. 59, and which I have not seen referred to by any Joyce commentator. I am indebted to James Sabben-

Clare for the stylish translation of this passage. To Gordon Pirie, Senior English Master of Winchester College, I am indebted for the quotation from Anthony Powell on p. 47, and to Professor Wallace Robson of Edinburgh University for the quotation from Reginald Farrer's lecture on Jane Austen, printed on p. 54.

I must also thank my son Michael Grose for his sharp if unfilial comments on many *bêtises* he detected in the manuscript; and my wife for putting up with my testiness and abstraction while the book, unworthy as it is, was being written.

K. H. G.

Acknowledgements

The author and publishers are indebted to the following for permission to quote from James Joyce's works and for the use of the illustrations: the Executors of the James Joyce Estate and the Society of Authors for all quotations and for the illustration of the corrected page proof of *Ulysses*; for extracts from *Ulysses* to the Bodley Head and Random House, Inc.; for excerpts from *A Portrait of the Artist as a Young Man*, copyright 1916 by B. W. Huebsch, copyright renewed 1944 by Nora Joyce, copyright 1964 by the Estate of James Joyce, reprinted by permission of the Viking Press Inc., and Jonathan Cape; to The Director of the National Library of Ireland, Dublin, for the photograph of the Library; to the Trustees of the British Museum for the photograph of James Joyce in academic dress, from the Harriet Weaver papers; to Miss Joan Budgen for the drawing of Joyce and Budgen; to the Trustees of the National Gallery for the cover portrait.

Editions Quoted in the Text

Dubliners: Penguin PB 1968
A Portrait of the Artist as a Young Man: Penguin PB 1969
Exiles: Signet Modern Classics PB 1968
Ulysses: Penguin PB 1969
Finnegans Wake: Faber & Faber 1971
Chamber Music: Cape PB 1972
Pomes Penyeach: Faber & Faber PB 1971

Contents

The Author

Kenneth Grose, M.A., was formerly an English Master at Winchester College. He is General Editor of the Literature in Perspective Series for which he has also collaborated in the volume on *Shakespeare*.

I

Joyce's Life and Times

How closely an author's works reflect his life is a perpetually fascinating field of study. Stephen Dedalus, Joyce's young hero and *alter ego*, produces a convincing demonstration of the correspondence between Shakespeare's life and his plays, in Chapter IX of *Ulysses*. It is possible, without much offence to credibility, to look at nearly all Joyce's work as autobiographical. 'What can a man know,' exclaimed James to his brother Stanislaus, 'but what passes inside his own head?' *A Portrait of the Artist as a Young Man*, *Exiles* and *Ulysses* are intensely subjective works. The two novels are so constructed that no other subject is possible, while the intimacy of his play *Exiles* is peculiarly self-revelatory.

If therefore we want to find out what Joyce thought and felt, we have only to read his work with understanding and sympathy. His life, too, is so well documented that it is easy to find out what he did. Apart from many references to him in the letters, essays and autobiographies of distinguished contemporaries—such as Yeats, Pound and Eliot—he has been exceptionally well served in the definitive biography of Richard Ellmann, which is a triumphant combination of myriads of facts and a witty and readable style. There are also the reminiscences of Joyce's brother Stanislaus, *My Brother's Keeper;* and of his artist friend Frank Budgen, who had the incredible fortune of meeting Joyce almost daily while he was composing *Ulysses.* Anyone interested in Joyce should read all three: this short sketch of his life draws heavily upon them.

James Joyce was born in 1882, the first of eleven surviving children of John Joyce, a talented but feckless 'good fellow' about Dublin. What little property John Joyce inherited he squandered; the downhill progress of the family fortunes is central to *A Portrait of the Artist*, and a recurrent theme in *Ulysses*, where Simon Dedalus appears several times, but rarely in an entirely flattering context. James seems to have been the only one of the children to respect his father; he shared the talent for singing, the love of drinking, and the ability to ignore the necessity for steady work at a paying job. The difference between them was that John Joyce devoted himself to drinking and good fellowship, whereas James neglected his family for his art, at any rate in his earlier years.

James was a clever and hardworking boy. His early education is fairly accurately told in *A Portrait*. He attended Clongowes Academy and Belvedere College, like Stephen Dedalus; but he also spent some time at the non-Jesuit Christian Brothers' school, not acknowledged in the 'fictional' work. Joyce greatly admired and respected his Jesuit teachers, for the most part; they certainly left their mark upon him. He did well in the national competitions which were the rungs of the educational ladder in those days. Like Stephen, he won exhibitions carrying sums like £30 (a useful amount in the nineties), with which he took the family out on extravagant sprees. We cannot doubt that his father encouraged this improvident expenditure; high living, even if only for one night, reinstated him among the well-to-do property-owning class.

From 1898–1902 James attended University College, Dublin; this was the Catholic counterpart of the ancient Protestant foundation, Trinity College, in rivalry to which it had been founded by Cardinal Newman in 1853. It was here that Gerard Manley Hopkins, a convert like Newman, had been Professor of Classics. Joyce took his degree in Languages, including Italian, which was to prove very useful to him in his exile. He was never an orthodox student; he read papers at College societies that dazzled and often enraged his fellows, he wrote a good deal of verse, and engaged in literary journalism. It was at this time that he began to write his 'epiphanies', those misleadingly named records of moments of revelation; the word usually means a showing forth of the divine, as in Christ's coming to earth at Christmas, but Joyce used it to denote moments when trivial incidents took on mystical significance—a revelation not of the extra-ordinary but of the ordinary. The contrast between his pale sentimental verse and the spare prose of these not very interesting stares at reality is marked; clearly it is in the prose epiphanies, if anywhere, that Joyce's originality expressed itself at this time.

Joyce tells in *A Portrait* of his long crisis of conscience concerning his religious life; he might well have become a priest, a Jesuit teacher, but he found he had no vocation. In fact, he did not leave the Church so much as change the Church for his Art: his devotion was directed into another channel, but ran just as strongly there for the rest of his life. Other objects of adoration he abjured. For instance, this was a time of a great upsurge of nationalism in Ireland, but Joyce rejected both the political and the literary sides of the movement. He felt out of sympathy with the aims of the Irish literary theatre, which began operations in 1899: its narrow poetical nostalgia for Ireland's legendary past and its preoccupation with peasants and aristocrats were both equally distasteful to him. The dominant figure in the international theatre was Ibsen, who was shocking conventional playgoers with his attempts to explore truly and with intense realism the springs of human conduct—he wrote about *drains*, they complained. Joyce championed the Norwegian dramatist in fierce debates in the College Literary and Historical Society, managed a triumphant publication of a notice of an Ibsen play in the *Fortnightly Review*, an influential London literary journal, and was honoured by a message from Ibsen himself. In 1900 he wrote an Ibsenian play about a young doctor, such as Joyce was then aiming to become. All the lines of his life were obviously leading him away from the provincial city and its preoccupations with itself. His choice of degree subjects—French and Italian—his interest in a dramatist of European status, his rejection of Irish nationalism, his contempt for the twilight world of Celtic legend, all this was turning him into an expatriate. Joyce did try very hard to establish himself in the Dublin literary world—as Stephen does in Chapter IX of *Ulysses*. A.E., George Russell, welcomed him to his circle, which included Yeats and George Moore. But their ways were not his; their polite literary parties and little coterie magazines did not accord with his independent touchy pride, his overweening sense of his own genius. To explore the cosmic significance of the trivialities of town life, to savour the pubs and brothels, to remain unwashed and clothed in lousy rags, to borrow small sums and cadge meals—these were his ways. In his scurrilous poem 'The Holy Office' he makes his position clear (see p. 42).

In October 1902 he began a course at the Catholic medical college, but soon found he hated it, so he left for Paris in December, largely on borrowed money, and managed to get himself enrolled for a medical course there. Here he lived from hand to mouth, sending to his impoverished home for money and clothes. He met Synge, the coming Irish playwright, and read for the first time the work of Dujardin, whom Joyce ever after credited with the invention of the interior monologue or 'stream of consciousness'. But (as with Stephen Dedalus in the beginning of *Ulysses*) he was called home to his mother's deathbed in April 1903; he again lived on small loans, disagreed with the editors who could have put work in his way, and did a little teaching (*Ulysses*, Chapter II). In early June 1904 he met Nora Barnacle, a lively, simple, unlettered girl, and on 16 June 1904—the day which became Bloomsday—he first walked out with her. He must have known that she was the only one for him, a complete foil to his proud, self-torturing, feckless spirit.

He was now writing *Stephen Hero*, the long autobiographical novel that later was condensed into *A Portrait of the Artist as a Young Man*; and at the instigation of Russell—though not to his prescription—he began to write the short stories which became *Dubliners*. But by the end of 1904 his dissatisfaction with the literary and social world of Dublin became obsessional, and after a memorable week in the Martello Tower of *Ulysses*, spent with Oliver St. John Gogarty (Buck Mulligan) and an Englishman who became the Haines of *Ulysses*, he persuaded Nora to go into exile with him unmarried. He had, he thought, obtained a post in Zürich, at one of the chain of Berlitz Language Schools; but he finally landed up in Trieste, then part of the Austro-Hungarian Empire. Here he was to remain until 1915, with interludes as a bank clerk in Rome and on visits to Ireland. He taught at more than one school, took private pupils, sang a little in public and a good deal in private, wrote newspaper articles on Ireland, and very often got drunk. His two children, Giorgio and Lucia, were born here, and he earned enough to have lived reasonably comfortably, had he managed the mundane details of living in a responsible way. Had it not been for the sober presence and dogged loyalty of brother Stanislaus, whom he had persuaded to come out in 1905, it is likely that the family would have gone under. James unashamedly sponged on Stanislaus, whose book, *My Brother's Keeper*, unfortunately deals only with their early Dublin years.

Two of Joyce's visits to Ireland were concerned with business. On one of them he had the remarkable job of agent for some Triestine business men who—at Joyce's instigation—tried to start the first public cinema in Ireland; the enterprise failed. On the second he tried in vain to get his collection of short stories, *Dubliners*, published. They had been accepted by Grant Richards in 1906, but the battle with both printer and publisher was protracted for many years; publication was delayed until 1914, when Joyce had acquired some reputation. Objections were made to disparaging remarks about King Edward VII in 'Ivy Day in the Committee Room' (p. 129), to unmistakable references to a homosexual in 'An Encounter', to the use of the swear-word 'bloody', and to the naming of actual people and pubs that could possibly be the subject of libel actions. But the true reason for the publisher's refusal (incredibly, after his accepting the book in the first place) seems to have been that the tone of the stories was denigratory of Ireland at a time of great national fervour. Joyce was finally so disgusted with the hostility shown him that after the abortive visit of 1912 he never set foot in Ireland again, not even to receive proffered honours when he became famous.

In 1913 two people of immense significance to him entered his life: Ezra Pound and, as a direct consequence, Harriet Weaver. Pound was the rich young American who was discovering new artists and poets in Europe, the herald of Modernism, the mentor of Yeats and T. S. Eliot. He happened to read a poem of Joyce's, and wrote asking for more. Joyce sent him *Dubliners* and portions of *A Portrait*, which Pound arranged to have published in a politico-literary magazine, *The Egoist*, of which Harriet Weaver was editor. This new fame made Grant Richards at last publish *Dubliners*, but the book made no money for its author for several years.

The outbreak of the Great War in 1914 put Joyce, as a British subject, into alien territory: Italian Trieste was a danger spot to its Austrian rulers anyway, and brother Stanislaus, who unlike James meddled in politics, was interned in Austria. James was allowed to move to Zürich; he could find no teaching work, but this neutral city attracted expatriates and agents from both sides of the conflict. Hence it was a lively city, watching the war and carrying on its intrigues from the side-lines. Joyce made many friends here, chief among whom was Frank Budgen, the English rover and painter, who talked to him daily about the new work on which he was now engaged. Budgen's book about *The Making of 'Ulysses'* is invaluable, the more so because Budgen was not a literary man so was able to discuss Joyce's ideas without preconceptions of what a novel should be.

Pound, himself a poet, knew well that to produce a masterpiece required absolute freedom for the writer to live his own life, think his own thoughts, and make his own experiments. It was fortunate, from this point of view, that Joyce had no teaching commitments; but he needed money, and Pound set about prompting Yeats, now influential in England, to arrange for a grant from the Royal Literary Fund, and later a Civil List pension. Two women also came anonymously to Joyce's rescue, assuring him a regular income. It was several years before Joyce discovered that one of them was Harriet Weaver, who continued to believe in him and saw his work into print, among all the persisting difficulties with squeamish printers and fainthearted publishers. Even Pound censored parts of the MSS he transmitted on Joyce's behalf to publishers.

Nevertheless, in 1916 *A Portrait* was published in America, along with *Dubliners*. But Joyce could persuade no one to perform or publish *Exiles*, the play about cuckoldry that he had written between finishing *A Portrait* and starting *Ulysses*. *Exiles* was not published till 1918, nor acted till 1919, when a German version made a weak impression in Munich. Meanwhile Joyce had helped to organise and manage the English Players, a semi-professional company who were to operate in Zürich and neighbouring Swiss towns. Their existence was precarious and stormy, and led Joyce into quarrels and litigation with British officials, on whom he revenged himself finally by immortalising them as Sgt.-Major Bennett and Private Carr, the foul-mouthed brute at the end of 'Circe', Chapter XV of *Ulysses*. Even Sir Horace Rumbold, the British Minister to Berne, has his name given to the illiterate Master Barber who applied for the job of public executioner (*Ulysses*, p. 301). One hardly knows whether to laugh or cry at genius's childish rages.

Other important events of his stay in Trieste were the beginning of his eye trouble, necessitating in 1917 the first of many operations, which probably did in the end more harm than good; and his brief and possibly platonic infatuation with Martha Fleischmann, who became the prototype of 'Henry Flower's' Martha (*Ulysses* p. 79), as well as the limping Gerty MacDowell of Chapter XIII.

The war over, in 1919 Joyce returned briefly to Trieste; but that city seemed stuffy and provincial after the international society of Zürich, and at Pound's instigation he moved to Paris, where he was to spend most of his remaining years. Here he gradually achieved the public recognition that he had always known was his due; he was soon the centre of an admiring circle of cultured friends. He had written about five-sixths of *Ulysses*; but there was as yet little hope of getting it published as one book—all the printers who were approached objected to the plain speaking about sexual matters, or were afraid of prosecution. It was being serialised in the American *Little*

Review; but this led to the journal being prosecuted and burned, and its editors were fined in New York. In Paris the climate was more favourable: and Miss Sylvia Beach, an American who ran an *avant-garde* bookshop to which she gave the name 'Shakespeare & Co.', decided to bring out the book. In order to publicise it, she arranged a séance, a lecture with readings, at her shop in 1921, and in February 1922, on Joyce's fortieth birthday, *Ulysses* was finally published—in spite of his infuriating habit of adding whole new passages and dozens of interlined phrases to the proofs: it is said that the book grew by one-third in size during the proof-reading. Naturally its reception was mixed. Many people found it obscene or incoherent; George Moore, the Irish literary pundit, whose novels are undeservedly neglected today, pronounced it infamous in style and in taste; Virginia Woolf called it 'underbred', a wonderfully expressive adjective that tells us a good deal about Virginia Woolf. But Yeats called it a work of genius, and Hemingway, then in Paris, said it was 'a great goddamn wonderful book'. It seemed that at last Joyce had arrived.

But life was never easy. He now began on *Finnegans Wake*, which was to occupy him for sixteen years, and on which he toiled in spite of increasing eye trouble that entailed surgical operations and long periods of darkness when he could compose only in his head. His family life became more turbulent, and on one occasion Nora left him to try living in Ireland with the children Giorgio and Lucia; fortunately for Joyce, the Civil War of 1923 and the operations of the I.R.A. drove her back to him. Opposition to his method—or madness—in this bizarre book caused friendships to fall off: brother Stanislaus, Harriet Weaver (who was still sending him money) and Pound all tried to show him that he was pursuing a course where no one could follow him. But he persevered; and in 1929 some supporters of his produced an apologia called *Our Exagmination round his Factification for Incamination of Work in Progress*; one chapter of the twelve was written by Samuel Beckett, another by William Carlos Williams. *Work in Progress* was the name given to excerpts from *Finnegans Wake* which were being published mainly in a new review called *transition*, and which aroused great interest in the literary world. At this time, too, *Ulysses* appeared in French and German translations, *Exiles* was produced in London (1926), *Pomes Penyeach*, a small collection of thirteen lyrics sold for a shilling in 1927, and a pirated American edition of *Ulysses* in 1926.

The next decade, however, brought more difficulties to the afflicted author. His father, whom we know well as Simon Dedalus, died in 1931, and his daughter Lucia showed the first symptoms of the schizophrenia that with his growing blindness was to make Joyce's last years a protracted agony. At first he insisted on his own treatment of her, having little faith in psychiatrists. From now until his death in 1941 she became increasingly unmanageable; he would not believe she was deranged, and kept her out of mental institutions with the help of friends and relations. But in the end she had to be confined, which afflicted him dreadfully—his paternal love made him consider her abandoned rather than cared for.

His work on *Finnegans Wake* continued to occupy all the rest of his mind, until its publication in 1939. Meanwhile *Ulysses* had survived a New York prosecution for obscenity in 1933, and was published unexpurgated in England (1936). Joyce was now in comfortable financial circumstances—or would have been had he not squandered his money in extravagances and his strength in drinking. His international fame was now assured, and when World War II broke out in 1939, he was distinguished enough to be allowed to leave France for Zürich, where he had spent World War I. He hardly had time to settle, with his son Giorgio, his grandson Stephen, and his wife Nora, before the stomach trouble that he had ignored, and refused to consult any doctor about, culminated in a perforated duodenal ulcer; he died soon after the operation on 13 January 1941.

His best epitaph is that of his long-suffering wife, who had never read his books; when asked about her acquaintance with the great literary figures who had come into her life, she replied, 'Sure, if you've been married to the greatest writer in the world, you don't remember all the little fellows.'

2

Dubliners

Joyce began these stories while he was still in Dublin, but most of them were written during the first months of exile; the original twelve stories were finished by the end of 1905 (he later added three), but he could not get them published without cuts and amendments until nine years later. Both publishers and printers (equally liable to prosecution under the laws of obscenity) were afraid to accept responsibility for such words as 'bloody', for references to homosexuality, for denigratory remarks about the new King Edward VII. But the general tone of the book, the unpatriotic candour of the grey picture of a drab, decaying city housing a mean, lack-lustre citizenry, sounded a discordant, even repellent, note in that time of growing Irish nationalism; and one suspects that much of the reluctance of the publisher, who had signed a contract with Joyce in 1906, but wrangled with him for eight years, can be attributed to this.

Joyce himself declared that he was trying to 'give Dublin to the world'; he wrote as he saw the plain truth; it was not his fault that an 'odour of corruption' remained in his nostrils even after he had moved to Trieste in 1904. Dublin might have been another Venice or another Christiania (which he idealised as his hero Ibsen's city) if it had housed a few truly cultured persons; but the purveyors of a false picture of an Ireland peopled only by Anglo-Irish aristocrats like Lady Gregory and the Syngean peasantry of *Riders to the Sea* he despised as romantic betrayers of the real Ireland, which he knew intimately and at first hand from his experiences of his own family and friends. Many of the characters in the stories are thinly disguised portraits of real people: his disreputable father, for instance, appears as the uncle in 'The Sisters' (p. 8) and 'Araby' (p. 31), the vile Farrington of 'Counterparts' (p. 84), Henchy in 'Ivy Day in the Committee Room' (p. 120), Kernan, the drunkard of 'Grace' (p. 148), and—perhaps more flatteringly—as Gabriel Conroy in 'The Dead' (p. 174). With such material, and such family life as is so vividly portrayed in *A Portrait*, it is not surprising that most of the stories, and particularly those he wrote first, are uncompromisingly harsh.

If Joyce was trying to gain sympathy for the Irish race, it is an odd way to set about it: 'Look how mean, how feckless, how unadventurous we are; this is the plain truth; do you still love us?' But it is in line with the dominant masochism of Joyce's character.

At the time of publication, 1914, the book aroused little enthusiasm: it sold slowly, and reviewers, apart from Ezra Pound, were curiously unmoved to praise. Readers are still puzzled today when they first open the book, although Joyce's method, which draws on Chekhov, is no longer new, and has been imitated by many subsequent short story writers. If you expect a 'story', with clearly presented characters engaged in unusual situations, moving by incidents to a climax or dénouement, you will indeed wonder whether you are reading anything of significance. For Joyce seldom makes any attempt to reach a climax; there is rarely a pay-off line. (An exception is 'Two Gallants', in which the depth of the depravity of the men is pointed in the last line (p. 58): 'A small gold coin shone in the palm'; and it becomes apparent that Corley is begging from the slavey he has seduced, while Lenehan, the other gallant, is hoping to share the proceeds.) In general there is no sense of striving for effect; any approach to an emotional climax will unaccountably lose momentum. The characters are not often explained or defined at the outset of the story (there are again partial exceptions, such as Mrs. Kearney in 'A Mother', p. 134, and Mr. James Duffy in 'A Painful Case', p. 105). They are made up, it seems, of odds and ends, bits of external appearance or internal temperament casually dropped on the table like jigsaw pieces. It is the reader who must do the work of assembling the pieces; and when he has made some sort of a picture, by deducing the missing details of a career or a past life, he has to pronounce his own moral judgment on it, for the author will not. Joyce presents us with a few sharp outlines, a few details the significance of which may not be immediately seen; he makes no insinuations; the inferences must be ours alone.

For instance, in the first page of 'A Painful Case' we read that Mr. James Duffy's room contains:

> a *black iron* bedstead, an *iron* wash-stand, four *cane* chairs, a clothes-*rack*, a *coal-scuttle*, a fender and *irons*, and a *square* table on which lay a double *desk*.

The hard comfortlessness of the room is made plain in the bare harshness of the words, echoed in the rest of the paragraph. It is thus no surprise to learn, on the next page, that Mr. Duffy 'lived at a little distance from his body', and that 'he never gave alms to beggars'. But Joyce does not *say* he was morally deficient: that inference must be the reader's. Joyce is not fired by a fierce indignation, like Swift, or a humane compassion, like Fielding, both anti-romantic realists. He is not a satirist, and never became one. These naturalistic stories are, as nearly as one can conceive, an impersonal record of very ordinary people in drab surroundings. They amount to an indictment of an entire city; if they tell the truth, then the streets and the people are uniformly mean.

The style, too, is deliberately flat and dull, like the subject-matter. Euphemisms, clichés and repetitions abound; not because Joyce knew no better, but because they are appropriate to his purpose. As he himself said, it is a style of 'scrupulous meanness'. Look at the last page of 'A Painful Case' (p. 114). Mr. James Duffy, the denizen of the uncarpeted room of p. 105, having refused human sympathy to the now dead Mrs. Sinico, realises his own loneliness; but he thinks in clichés: 'he felt that he had been outcast from life's feast' (a neat contrast, incidentally, to his usual frugal meal of corned beef and cabbage, p. 110); and the phrase is repeated five lines later. The deadness of the words is emphasised by the metaphor of the first half of the sentence: 'he *gnawed* the rectitude of his life', a masterly verb which extends the metaphor of the feast, and thus ties up beautifully with the cliché; and with the word *rectitude* the 'square table with its double desk' of the first page clicks into place. Mrs. Sinico had drunkenly walked on to the railway lines, and that same evening a disappearing train, likened to 'a worm with a fiery head winding through the darkness', insistently beats the rhythm of her name as it recedes from him; then the last few lines descend to a flatness which carefully avoids any emotional tug at the heart-strings:

> He waited for some minutes listening. He could hear nothing: the night was perfectly silent. He listened again; perfectly silent. He felt that he was alone.
>
> p. 115

Scrupulous meanness is in evidence everywhere in the fifteen stories, which are arranged in a careful sequence. The original twelve were planned in four groups of three. 'The Sisters', 'An Encounter' and 'Araby' are set in 'my' childhood; they are told in the first person. 'Eveline', 'After the Race' and 'The Boarding House' Joyce called stories of adolescence: the main characters are not fully adult. The next three (of the twelve) are 'Counterparts', 'Clay' and 'A Painful Case', with fully grown-up people and problems. In the fourth group, 'Ivy Day in the Committee Room', 'A Mother' and 'Grace', Joyce moves into the wider life of Dublin, placing the action in local politics, local musical circles and the Catholic Church. Thus he brought to fruition his intention, formed with the first story of the book, and the first to be written, of revealing the paralysis that gripped the soul of the city. After the book was completed and accepted for publication, he added two stories which reinforce the original message: 'Two Gallants' and 'A Little Cloud', the second of which is a terrifying glimpse into the intimate hatred of an inadequate marriage. He also wrote that remarkable self-revelation, 'The Dead', which ends the collection on a somewhat more poetical note, while still maintaining its bleak exposure of Dublin.

Dubliners is thus a complete work of art, not a mere chance collection. Themes and symbols recur. Grey and brown are the dominant colours, light and dark alternate, father and mother are never far away. The over-riding theme of paralysis is stated on the first page, where the old demented priest is in the grip of it; the feeling of moral paralysis, or of lack of will-power, or of frustrated hopes (a paralysis of the developing possibilities of life) is ever present, whether in Eveline (p. 34) who cannot bring herself to take the decisive step towards the new world; in Mr. Kernan (p. 148) who cannot break the grip of alcohol in spite of petitions for grace to enable him to do so; or in poor Maria ('Clay', p. 97), whose low intelligence matches her low stature— though she at least is not unsympathetically portrayed.

Finally, on the very last page, Joyce provides a vision of the snow softly falling, not only over the Gresham Hotel in Dublin where a man has come to a full realisation of the lack of vitality in his marriage and in himself, but also falling over the whole land of Ireland, obliterating the landmarks and reducing all individual features to a uniform shapelessness, covering both the living and the dead, who are thus equated.

But the last story is different from the others in many ways. First, it is considerably longer and contains more movement and more people than the others. Joyce realised after he had written fourteen stories that his picture was too gloomy, possibly because he had omitted one important feature of Dublin life, its tradition of hospitality. So he created a great New Year Party, a much larger and superficially more cheerful affair than the family Christmas dinner that is so marvellously described in *A Portrait of the Artist as a Young Man*. Most of the characters are drawn from life: the Misses Morkan, whose party it is, and their niece, are Joyce's aunts and cousin, and their house is described much as it really was. His father, John Joyce, carved the goose just as Gabriel Conroy has to; and Gabriel's complimentary after-dinner speech is, according to brother Stanislaus, just such a speech as his father made at these occasions.

But apart from the atmosphere of movement on an ampler canvas, and of an attempt at conviviality (however frustrated or pathetic), which sets the story apart from the other fourteen, it is

remarkable for its autobiographical element. Gabriel Conroy
may have borrowed his oration and his actions, his turn of
speech and gestures from John Joyce, but his psychological
make-up is pure James. The circumstances of their lives are
similar: Gabriel is a language teacher and a writer who has spent
much time abroad; he is also an intellectual who finds he cannot
surrender to life, but must torment himself with doubt about
the quality of his own emotions, of his achievements and even
of his marriage. His wife, Gretta, is amazingly near Nora
Barnacle: she too came from the unsophisticated west of Ireland,
she too was comparatively uneducated, and she too mourned—
at least Joyce was convinced she did—for a lover in Galway who
shared both the name Michael and the circumstances of his early
death with Gretta's Michael Furey. Joyce's poem 'She weeps
over Rahoon' is about Nora's grief for her Galway Michael;
and its close verbal correspondence to the last page of 'The
Dead' underlines the connection; the lines:

> 'Rain on Rahoon falls softly, softly falling,
> Where my dark lover lies.'   POMES PENYEACH, p. 16

have clear echoes in:

> 'It was falling ... falling softly ... softly falling ... where Michael
> Furey lay buried ... faintly falling ... upon all the living and
> dead.'   DUBLINERS, p. 220

In this story Joyce is making his first attempt to externalise
one of his most dominant obsessions—with, to put it baldly,
cuckoldry. It was not that he really thought Nora was physically
unfaithful to him, but his jealous soul wanted to be sure that she
loved him and him alone; he could never come to terms with the
thought that her love might have been given to someone else
before she had met him. That his mind constantly revolved the
question of women's constancy, of the permanence of love, is
demonstrated by the recurrence of the notion in *Ulysses*, where
Bloom's masochistic delight in Boylan's conquest of his wife
Molly (p. 507) is only the culmination of the preoccupation with
her unfaithfulness that he has experienced throughout the day. It

23

is not an uncommon subject in literature; apart from famous exemplars of sexual jealousy in *Othello* and *The Winter's Tale*, there is the penetrating study of the jealous Faulkland, the power of whose mental agonies is too deep to make a fit subject for laughter in Sheridan's *The Rivals*, which cheerful comedy it almost ruins; there Lydia Languish and her romantic notions cannot be taken seriously, while the anguish of Faulkland is all too real.

Bloom, however, finds consolation in resignation (see p. 122), and Gabriel Conroy feels generous tears fill his eyes as his hitherto selfish and domineering love for Gretta acquires a new dimension of sympathy. This was a state of mind that obsessed Joyce, and he tried to express it even more clearly in his play *Exiles*, which will be discussed in Chapter 4.

3

A Portrait of the Artist as a Young Man

Probably the most frequently read and most keenly enjoyed of Joyce's work, this book is a re-writing of a long—very long—autobiographical novel called *Stephen Hero*, which itself had begun in 1904 as a short story called 'A Portrait of the Artist'; on its rejection by the magazine *Dana* (see p. 90) Joyce, encouraged by 'A.E.', began to reconstruct and expand it as he started his exile. For the first three years he went on adding to it until it grew to over 300,000 words; but in 1907 he realised that it was becoming too diffuse, and started to re-model it into the tightly organised medium-length novel of five chapters that we now have under almost the original title. *Stephen Hero* can be read in a version which has lost some of the early pages and was not published until 1944; but except to those who like delving into the circumstances of an author's life, or comparing successive versions, it is hardly worth the trouble. *A Portrait of the Artist as a Young Man* covers the same ground in a much more significant way; among many omissions in the shorter version, perhaps the most striking is the reduction to a very minor role of Stanislaus—Maurice—who was the admiring yet critical brother whom Joyce called Stephen's 'whetstone'. Hardly surprisingly, Stanislaus was not pleased.

A Portrait is the story, told in episodic form, of Stephen Dedalus's early life. Its title suggests that it is concerned with the development of Stephen as an artist, or rather as poet and novelist; and theories of aesthetics are discussed at some length in Chapter 5. But the main interest to many readers is the gradual emergence of Stephen's conviction that in order to survive as an artist he must shake himself loose from the fetters of Church, Country and Family, and seek exile in order to be free to 'forge in the smithy of my soul the uncreated conscience of my race', as he declares on the last page.

So the forging of the fetters, and their nature, occupy the earlier pages. Chapter I is mainly concerned with his first school, the Jesuit academy for well-to-do boys at Clongowes. The first two pages present vivid sensual impressions of babyhood, couched in the sort of language fond parents use when talking to infants (pp. 7-8); their significance as an introduction is that certain key themes are touched on: his love of words and music; his family and friends—his father's rather pretentious monocle, his great-uncle Charles, and Dante, the Mrs. Riordan with whom Leopold Bloom tried to ingratiate himself (*Ulysses*, p. 659); and the political situation in Ireland epitomised in the two brushes, one green-backed and one maroon-backed, that Dante kept in her wardrobe (p. 7).

Three episodes follow. The first (pp. 8-27) deals with his early days at Clongowes, his fears of the dormitory light going out before he had finished his prayers at his chilly bedside, his bewilderment among the bigger and rougher fellows, and his semi-delirious dream of the death of Parnell (p. 27). The second episode is a brilliant evocation of a family Christmas dinner which begins as a sumptuous feast, but ends in political argument and violent recriminations. The gradual build-up of emotion, fed with alcohol on the side of the Irish nationalist Mr. Casey and outraged religious bigotry on the part of Dante, is enthralling; this is possibly the most vivid scene in the book, with its careful control of detail and symbol. The bone of contention is the betrayal of Parnell, the Irish national leader at Westminster, by the hierarchy of the Catholic Church, who rejected him when his adulterous affair with Kitty O'Shea became public (see pp. 144-5). For Joyce, the conflict expressed the unreasoning antipathy of Church and State, both of which were demonstrably unable to provide a settled base for a seeker after truth.

In the last section of Chapter I Stephen and his schoolfellows discuss the harsh punishments at that time meted out to naughty boys. During the ensuing lesson Stephen is unjustly caned by the prefect of studies—*anglice* the headmaster—whose terror-striking, bullying behaviour reeks to a modern mind of sexual repression. Stephen, greatly daring, complains to the rector, who is that Father Conmee whom we meet again in *Ulysses*, notably Chapter X, 'The Wandering Rocks'. His complaint is upheld, but later the Jesuit priests had a good laugh together over the incident (pp. 70–3)—though some of Simon Dedalus's anti-clerical bias and love of a good story must be discounted before the masters can be accused of callousness. No doubt the draconian Father Dolan devoured fewer defenceless schoolboys in consequence, at any rate for a time.

The heroic innocence of Stephen does not live long; in Chapter II, with the family's move from the idyllic Blackrock suburb into Dublin, forced on them by his father's fecklessness, he attains adolescence and is soon eating of the tree of carnal knowledge. This chapter has six episodes, in most of which Stephen's growing sexuality is balanced against the descent of the family. Stephen at Blackrock (pp. 60–5) is painted as a boy who enjoys his own solitary yearnings, though he has friends to play with and plenty of activity to engage in including helping the milkman on his round, as little Archie does in *Exiles*. In the second episode (pp. 65–70) come several disconnected flashes of his new, more sordid, life, ending in his first innocent encounters with a girl, Emma Cleary, who might have been revealed as the ideally beautiful Mercedes he imagined as he read Dumas. His experiences in his new Jesuit academy—Belvedere—where he has been awarded a free place, are not exactly congenial. The fourth episode (pp. 73–87) is ostensibly concerned with the School play; but Stephen is on the one hand bantered by the arrogant boy-about-town Heron, and on the other is tormented by the presence of Emma with his parents in the audience. He is also accused of heresy by a bigoted master, and is roughed up by a gang of his new schoolfellows for declaring that the heretic Byron was the greatest poet, not the milk-and-water Tennyson later mockingly described as 'Lawn Tennyson' in *Ulysses*. It is fitting that Stephen should champion an exiled poet, an immoral Cain-like figure, and suffer for it.

A visit to Cork with his father, who was selling the last remains of his inheritance, leads on to the painful final section (pp. 96–101) in which the extreme fecklessness of the family is amply demonstrated. What sort of a father allows—encourages even—his son to spend the money he has won in examinations on taking them all out to dinner, on delicacies from the most expensive city grocery stores, and on expeditions to the theatre, in a 'swift season of merrymaking'? To point the extravagance of his conduct, he 'wrote out resolutions', put his books in order and began to paint his bedroom with pink enamel paint—until, neat symbol, the pot of paint ran out (p. 98).

> He had tried to build a breakwater of order and elegance against the sordid tide of life without him and to dam up, by rules of conduct and active interests and new filial relations, the powerful recurrence of the tides within him.

He fell into what Catholics call 'mortal sin', and as he wanders the maze of narrow dirty streets (later to be the locale of 'Night-town' in Chapter XV of *Ulysses*) he is seduced by a prostitute.

Chapter III begins as Chapter II ends, in the sordid streets; his soul is 'going forth to experience, unfolding itself sin by sin' (p. 103). Now comes the climax of his religious life; at school he is a leading figure in the sodality of the Blessed Virgin Mary, but on his lips as he softly murmurs her liturgical names in the holy office lingers 'the savour itself of a lewd kiss' (p. 105). Clearly the turmoil of his soul cannot continue, and the three terrifying sermons preached by Father Arnall (the sympathetic understanding schoolmaster-priest from Clongowes, pp. 47 ff) force Stephen into confession of his sins. The chapter ends (p. 146) in a blaze of pure whiteness: an invisible grace 'makes light' his limbs, his soul is 'made fair', the kitchen lamp casts a 'tender shade', white pudding and eggs are on the shelf, he walks to communion 'in the quiet morning', the flowers are fragrant and white on the altar, and the pale flames of the candles are 'clear and silent as his own soul'.

Now follows a period of extravagantly scrupulous holiness, in which his senses—all of them—are mortified, and his natural animal pleasure in them thwarted, in an attempt to conquer the flesh. The first section of Chapter IV (pp. 147–53) describes with acute perception the self-tortures of the over-religious mind.

> A restless feeling of guilt would always be present with him . . .
> Perhaps that first hasty confession wrung from him by the fear of
> hell had not been good?

His devotion is now so obvious to all that he is, quite properly and scrupulously, asked by the director of the college to consider whether he has a vocation for the religious life. He is naturally proud at being explicitly singled out, and in his imagination the life of a priest—the Reverend Stephen Dedalus, Society of Jesus—is idealised (pp. 158–9); he is almost flattered into acceptance. But after the interview as he says goodbye at the priest's door he hears music coming from

> a quartet of young men . . . striding along with linked arms, sway-
> ing their heads and stepping to the agile melody of their leader's
> concertina . . . Smiling at the trivial air he raised his eyes to the
> priest's face and . . . detached his hand slowly which had acquiesced
> faintly in the companionship.

The moment is crucial, the action symbolic. Stephen makes his decision.

> His destiny was to be elusive of social or religious orders . . . He
> was destined to learn his own wisdom apart from others or to learn
> the wisdom of others himself wandering among the snares of the
> world.   p. 162

And the world obtrudes itself as soon as he gets home to his family, its squalid tea-table and the news of yet another impending removal to even deeper squalor. But the children sing together; their music, telling of human joys and sorrows, is the music of earth, of people who need companionship in their weariness and pain (p. 164). He cannot be satisfied with 'the pale service of the altar'; it is a few days later that the cries of his bantering schoolfellows: 'Stephanos Dedalos! Bous Stephanoumenos! Bous Stephaneforos! (Crown-bearing ox!)' announce his destiny to him. Not only is he the 'hawk-like man flying sunward above the sea', but also the sacrificial ox who wears a crown or garland as sign of his dedication to the gods. Stephen realises (in a palpitating passage on p. 169) what his life so far had been leading him towards. He may soar above the clouds but his material must be 'the sluggish matter of the earth'. It is at that moment that he sees the wading girl, whom he does not know and to whom he does not speak; but her image as of a mortal angel, rather than of the Virgin Mary, calls to him to enter the fair courts of life, with the certainty of human error but also the hope of glory (p. 172).

It is in this chapter, too, that his interest in words as objects with a life of their own becomes apparent to him. Right from the start of his life he has been a manipulator of words. Now he knows that if he is ever to express both the glowing sensible world and the inner world of individual emotions, it must be with words (p. 167).

By the end of Chapter IV, then, Stephen has made one crucial decision: he has substituted art for religion, or rather he has made art his religion. An ordinary man's rejection of a call to the priesthood would in no way entail a rejection of the Church and of the orthodox Christian way of life; but Joyce was a passionate man who did nothing by halves. He was to devote his life, his present and his future family, his friends and his career, to the long and bitter labour of writing. Such devotion is rarely seen in religious people; it is the mark of the saint. It was inculcated into him, no doubt, by the discipline and example of the Jesuits who formed his mind and whom he never ceased to respect. James Joyce is more closely integrated into Stephen Dedalus in Chapter V than anywhere else in this book or in the later *Ulysses*, where a certain detachment can be observed; as Wordsworth saw a waterfall 'frozen by distance'. A good deal of this chapter is concerned, like the preceding four, with the external circumstances of Stephen's existence: the feckless family sinking further into squalor (pp. 173–5); his friendship with fellow-students such as Davin, the Irish peasant patriot (pp. 180–3, 201–3); his visit to the National Theatre (p. 226); student chaff and protests (pp. 194, 230–1, 236); the cracking of a louse (p. 233); the very funny account of a physics lecture from the point of view of unruly students, who existed even in those days (pp. 190–4); and so on. These episodes (now run together in long sections, not separated as in the earlier chapters) are necessary to provide a living background to Stephen's mental and spiritual development, which is laid bare in three specially significant encounters.

The first is with the dean of studies (pp. 184–90). The leading dons at University College were, of course, Jesuits like the brothers at Clongowes and Belvedere, and the dean is following in the tradition of Newman and Hopkins, both English converts and both more than nominally alien in Ireland. The foreignness of the dean is brought to Stephen's notice by his use of the simple word 'funnel' for what Stephen called a 'tundish', a utensil for pouring liquid into narrow-necked receptacles. Stephen's dissatisfaction with an Ireland dominated by the English does not seek action in the political nationalism of Davin and the Sinn Fein, or in the literary nationalism of the new theatrical venture that became the Abbey Theatre; he did not reject the English language but, as Shakespeare did, took it and bent it to his own purpose. To do this he had to leave the land where the struggle was motivated by provincial rather than universal considerations. An art such as Stephen's could not flourish in the shallow soil of nationalism; paradoxically, his love of his country could only be freely expressed in an exile which allowed him to escape also from those who did not know what a tundish was, as well as from those who were ignorant of funnels. His dislike of the condescending dean, a mere convert, later blossoms into outright hatred of the invading folklore-hunter Haines, the Englishman in the early chapters of *Ulysses*.

In a second long conversation (pp. 204–15), Stephen walks with his irreverent friend Lynch as he expounds his own aesthetic theory, an individual version of the doctrine of St.

Thomas Aquinas, the great 13th-century Catholic philosopher, who reconciled Aristotle's precepts with those of Christianity. Stephen's main purpose is to work towards a definition of the 'aesthetic emotion'—what happens to you when you feel pleasure at the contemplation of a work of art. A string of statements embodied his conclusions:

> Art is the human disposition of sensible or intelligible matter for an aesthetic end. p. 207
>
> That is beautiful the apprehension of which pleases. p. 207
>
> The true and the beautiful are akin. p. 207
>
> The first step in the direction of beauty is to understand the frame and scope of the imagination. p. 208
>
> Three things are needed for beauty; wholeness, harmony and radiance. p. 211

He gives clear definitions of these last three qualities on pp. 212–13, and ends his exposition with a remarkable paragraph in which he declares that the artist must, like the God of creation, remain behind his work and not be personally recognisable in its surface. The novelist or dramatist creates personages from the material of his experience of life; but his personages are not himself. In other words, Shakespeare is neither Iago nor Othello.

This passage is often taken to mean that Joyce remained impersonally in the background of both *A Portrait* and *Ulysses*, as he obviously does in most of the stories in *Dubliners*. True, he looks on his younger self with a cold clinical eye; the Stephen of both books is not indulgently treated. 'Dedalus, you're an antisocial being, wrapped up in yourself', says McCann on p. 177. 'An impossible person', says Buck Mulligan on p. 15 of *Ulysses*. But stand aside he cannot. Stephen Dedalus's mind is the mind of James Joyce; and similarly Leopold Bloom's thoughts are the thoughts of his creator, his *alter ego*. This is the paradox of dramatic creation: Shakespeare is both Iago and Othello.

The reader is not asked to swallow all this philosophical speculation in one indigestible lump. By having the irreverent interlocutor Lynch inject scurrilous quips and ask for cigarettes, by outlining the course of the walk through the streets, by letting another student friend, Donovan, interrupt the conversation (pp. 210–1), Joyce not only lightens the texture but makes indirect comments which prove to be apposite—such as Donovan's remarks about the Laocoön, to which Stephen was to allude three pages later. (The German critic Lessing called his exposition of aesthetics after the famous group of statuary figures depicting the death of Laocoön and his sons, as described in Virgil's *Aeneid*.) It is of course necessary, when making a portrait of an artist, to discuss and establish the principles of the artist's work; Stephen, in rejecting the Church, embraces Art: he requires, he says, 'a new terminology and a new personal experience' (p. 209).

In the second long section of this chapter his sensibilities are shown at work; his search for self-expression through the medium of words is pursued. Stephen thinks of the girl who has rejected or ignored him, links her with the Church that is too closely tied up with narrow nationalism, and allows his imagination to take flight in words, as did his namesake Daedalus with self-made wings (p. 225). If the poem he writes is pale and precious, it is of the same kind as all Joyce's lyrical poems, and we can only be thankful that the Poet's cloak is merely the Artist's fictional disguise. The Artist that Joyce developed into was to be a novelist, not a lyrical poet, though parts of his mature work, especially *Finnegans Wake*, are poetry rather than fiction.

From page 238 Stephen has his third decisive encounter: Cranly, a subtle disputant, tries to reconcile him to his home, his country and his religious vows. But Stephen declares, as Satan did, 'I will not serve' (p. 239), and on p. 245 the final decision, to go into exile, is announced, to be clearly stated in its full implication on p. 247:

> I will try to express myself in some mode of life or art as freely as I can and as wholly as I can, using for my defence the only arms I allow myself to use—silence, exile, and cunning . . .
> And I am not afraid to make a mistake, even a great mistake, a lifelong mistake, and perhaps as long as eternity too.

One might expect the book to end here: the portrait is complete—even down to the lice on his unwashed neck (p. 233). Yet there are still six pages of extracts from Stephen's journal, containing many trivialities and unexplained references. Edward Garnett, who read the manuscript for Duckworth the publisher in 1916, called it 'a complete falling to bits; the pieces of writing and the thoughts are all in pieces and they fall like damp, ineffective rockets'. Many readers are equally puzzled. It certainly seems a flat ending.

It does, however, enable Joyce to tie up some loose ends in an economical way, to bring together some of the themes and symbols that have been formative influences on Stephen's mind—such as the unnamed girl's rejection of him, the dean's tundish, his monocled father's proprietorial hopes for his future, and his mother's practical concern for his welfare. It is also a move towards the new technique, interior monologue, or stream of consciousness, that is to be developed to its most elaborately expressive form in *Ulysses*. And finally, it culminates in a somewhat grandiose aspiration, in which some critics have found that Joyce is making implied strictures on the callow young man by making him appear pretentious and absurd:

Welcome, O life! I go to encounter for the millionth time the reality of experience and to forge in the smithy of my soul the uncreated conscience of my race.

Old father, old artificer, stand me now and ever in good stead.

p. 253

To my mind, this is not a send-up. Stephen, with all his arrogance and pride, is a dedicated priest of the imagination. So was Joyce; his whole life was devoted to his art, and he took himself as seriously as any genius must. There is no room for doubt in the devouring passion of creative activity. By the time Joyce had finished his ten-year labour on the book, he had grown old enough to see that the 'impossible', solipsistic Stephen needed (as his mother prays that he will, in the sentence immediately preceding the apostrophe to life, quoted above) to learn 'what the heart is and what it feels'. This is the subject-matter of *Ulysses*, and to achieve a more humane revelation of it he has to create Bloom and Molly; in them, rather than in the intellectual Stephen Dedalus, is the word made flesh. But the artist who stands behind his creation must partake of the nature of godhead, and gods are not modest.

4

Exiles

Critics have called this play nasty, incomprehensible, confusing and confused, a sad anti-climax. It certainly does not make for easy or pleasant reading; on the page it is overwhelmingly cerebral and narrow, and over-mechanical in the contrivances by which the four (or three-and-a-half) main characters are always presented in twos, engaged in soul-searching dialogues in which they seem to succeed only in mystifying each other as well as the reader.

But in the theatre *Exiles* has a deep and reverberant effect. Richard Rowan, the returned exile, is a curiously obsessive figure; his powerful, passionate mind is shown seeking to carry its search for freedom into new territories of feeling, and though we may finally think him mad, we have learnt to sympathise with him, and to feel sorry for the simple, warm, innocent Bertha whom he torments even more than he torments himself. In this respect the play is intensely absorbing, and deeply satisfying, as those who saw the Royal Shakespeare Company's production in London in 1971 will witness. The producer was Harold Pinter, who induced on the stage a menacing atmosphere of psychological claustrophobia such as that which characterises some of his own plays.

Again, the play draws on Joyce's own experience. Clearly the returned exiles are Joyce himself and his wife Nora, already delineated in the 'country-cute' Gretta Conroy of 'The Dead'. Little Archie, their eleven-year-old son, calls his father *babbo*, as Giorgio Joyce did, and delights in going off to ride with the milkman as young Stephen did in *A Portrait* (p. 63). There are several of these minor correspondences; what is more important is that Joyce is externalising in Richard his own psychological hang-ups.

Richard and Bertha Rowan have returned to Dublin from twelve years of exile, during which Richard, a philosopher and writer, has acquired enough reputation to make him a strong candidate for a chair at the University. He is welcomed back by his old friend and intellectual sparring partner Robert Hands, who has degenerated into a journalist and man of the world, a frankly hedonistic bon-vivant and lady-killer. Robert not only writes eulogies of Richard in the Irish press, not only fixes the academic appointment, but makes passes at Bertha, who naturally and unself-consciously enjoys his attentions. The question appears to be whether Robert will succeed in getting Bertha into bed with him: a conventional dramatic triangle, perhaps with the position only slightly complicated by Robert's attractive and educated cousin Beatrice, with whom Richard has been conducting soulful correspondence during his absence, and who is obviously very much in love with him.

But the relationship of these people is by no means a conventional dramatic triangle or quadrilateral, because two of the people are not ordinary people—or at least they do not display the ordinary generalised emotions of popular domestic tragi-comedy. Richard and Bertha have been living together as man and wife, yet have not marrried. In Richard's view, subjecting their love and devotion to an external authority, civil or religious, would have been sacrilege; to Bertha, love and motherhood are complete in themselves—like Molly Bloom later, she is 'the earth, dark, formless mother, darkly conscious of her instincts', as the author himself says in the notes he wrote for the play (p. 153). The intense desire of Richard is expressed in his last speech: 'To hold you by no bonds, even of love, to be united with you body and soul in utter nakedness.' This renunciation of 'bonds' makes him also renounce the usual moral sanctions of husband (though he is *not* technically a husband) against adulterer. He wants to try Bertha in the fire of Robert's commonplace passion. He deliberately encourages her to go to him in his conventional love-nest, with its perfume spray and its pink-shaded lights; he again and again makes it clear to her that she has complete freedom to surrender to her natural desires—for Robert is an attractive and skilful wooer, and knows how to soothe and flatter her.

To Robert, love means above all else sexual attraction; it is consummated in physical union (p. 78). To Richard, it is a union of souls. As Joyce says in his notes (p. 149):

> The soul like the body may have a virginity. For the woman to yield it or for the man to take it is the act of love. Love . . . is in fact so unnatural a phenomenon that it can scarcely repeat itself, the soul being unable to become virgin again . . .

It seems that in spite of Bertha's utter surrender to him, even to the extent of accepting his unconventional refusal to set the seal of 'respectability' on the union, Richard is tortured by doubts as to whether Bertha's soul has truly yielded its virginity to him; and by the end of the play it is clear that he never will cease to torture himself:

> RICHARD (*still gazing at her and speaking as if to an absent person*): I have wounded my soul for you—a deep wound of doubt which can never be healed.   p. 148

Nobody but a saint or a simpleton could live with such a man; and Bertha is something of both. She is armoured with a proud integrity that is only momentarily pierced by jealousy of the girl who is Richard's intellectual and aesthetic inspiration, Beatrice, who is his Muse as her namesake was Dante's. Bertha's integrity is not compromised by her feelings of affection and gratitude to Robert, the seducer bringing gifts symbolised by the red roses (p. 25), like Blazes Boylan with his red carnation in *Ulysses*, 'The toff with a flower in his mouth,' and one feels it would not be compromised even if she did go to bed with him. As a matter of fact, Joyce does not tell whether she did or not.

But Richard can be understood only in terms of morbid psychology; he is a sick man; his wound will never heal. Like Bloom, he is a masochist. This is first revealed by his intense detailed cross-examination of Bertha in pp. 56–60. He himself tells Robert that he longed to be betrayed by him and Bertha (p. 87). He also describes how in their early years he had once woken Bertha to tell her of his own betrayal of her with a prostitute: 'She must know me as I am' (p. 83). He puts into practice the maxim '*Tout comprendre, c'est tout pardonner*', but in an inverted sense; he takes it to mean that one can't forgive *unless* one knows everything, that *total* confession is a necessity. (One is reminded of the stark truth of *Dubliners*, see p. 19.)

This behaviour is, then, abnormally masochistic; it is not presented in a comic way, as later it is worked into *Ulysses*. The play is no more a comedy than *Hedda Gabler* or *When We Dead Awaken*, those Ibsen naturalistic dramas with which it has such close affinities. It is hard to find a laugh, or even a smile, in it. The series of face-to-face interviews is deadly serious; even the little boy Archie, who might have brought a ray of archly sentimental sunshine, is used as a missile.

Like the master Ibsen's plays, *Exiles* has its symbols; I have already mentioned the roses, out of which a good deal of mileage is extracted. There is also the smooth, cool unimpressionable solipsistic stone (p. 47), which appears to stand for woman as a sex object. ('Do you think I am a stone?' cries Bertha on p. 130.) The rain that falls reminds us of the rain that falls on Rahoon (see p. 23), or the snow at the end of 'The Dead'. But what is the significance of the 'fresh Dublin Bay herrings', cried offstage by a fish-woman at the climax of Act III (p. 139)? Is there some subtle hint at the early Christian fish symbol, linking Bertha or Richard with Christ as a sacrificial figure? Or is it merely an irrelevant naturalistic detail in the manner of Chekhov? Whatever it signifies, it is not made explicit; and this may be regarded as a blemish, since it does not illuminate the action as a dramatic symbol should.

The title *Exiles* is in itself a verbal symbol. Of course, Richard and Bertha are returned exiles, and one part of the message of the play is that Ireland cannot easily welcome back those who have felt their intellectual and artistic freedom cannot flourish in Dublin's atmosphere of literary, ecclesiastical and political bigotry. Robert, the skilful journalist accustomed to sounding public opinion, gives expression to the general feelings of Dublin people towards Richard in his article quoted on p. 129. There can be little doubt that Joyce meant the words to apply to his own case, especially as they are adapted from a review of *Chamber Music* by one of his own old friends, Thomas Kettle. In sending Richard home he is fulfilling in fiction his own frustrated wish: for Joyce was never to live in Ireland, never to be acclaimed as the creator of his country's conscience, never to be appointed to a professorship; and as I said on p. 13, when he was famous he refused the honour of membership of the Irish Academy.

But Richard and Bertha are exiles in a deeper sense. They are exiled, through Richard's intransigent idealism, from the comfortable conventions that make life bearable for ordinary mortals. Where the rules of conduct have daily to be forged anew in soul-searching and soul-searing encounters, men and women are frighteningly alone. Surrounding society speaks as strange a language as any foreign tongue. Although Joyce suggests in his notes that Robert might go into exile (p. 157), it is the frightening isolation of Richard and Bertha that is the keynote of the play's final cadence.

What then remains the dominant impression after 'three cat and mouse acts' (p. 157)? First, a feeling of frustration in that the reader does not know the answer to two or three problems that the play has been propounding. Did Bertha and Robert commit adultery? Would it have pleased or enraged Richard if he knew that they had? Had the bizarre notion, implicit in Bertha's actions and made explicit in the notes, that she might reconcile the two men through her body, not just through normal friendship, ever any chance of succeeding? Does Robert go away into exile, as he intended, or does Richard take Bertha into exile again, having refused or not been given his chair in the University?

Possibly Joyce would have regarded these questions as naïve. None of his books reaches a tidy conclusion. A more positive impression we are left with is that of a powerful emotional personality in Richard Rowan, a man tormented by the inability of body to live up to the highest aspirations of soul. For him, the flesh is indeed weak. He cannot console himself, as Donne does in 'The Ecstasie', by recognising the paramount necessity for the existence of the body as a vehicle for the soul to express and communicate its motions:

> So must pure lovers soules descend
>   T' affections, and to faculties,
> Which sense may reach and apprehend,
>   Else a great Prince in prison lies.
> T' our bodies turne wee then, that so
>   Weake men on love reveal'd may looke;
> Loves mysteries in soules doe grow,
>   But yet the body is his booke.

John Donne: THE ECSTASIE

It is no wonder, then, that Ezra Pound, on reading the play, pronounced it unfit for the stage. He didn't believe an audience could follow it or take it in, even if anyone were bold enough to stage it in 'our chaste and castrated English-speaking world'. Anything requiring thought, said Pound, could not appeal to the mass. There can be no doubt that *Exiles* will never appeal to the mass: what great drama does? But audiences have grown up since his day; people who can take Samuel Beckett and Harold Pinter find little difficulty in understanding *Exiles*; and to see it well performed, or to hear it on the radio, for which it is peculiarly well suited, is to undergo an absorbing experience.

5

Joyce's Verse

Joyce wrote verse during his whole life, and especially in his early years. A good deal of it was comic and satirical; he was expert at composing limericks and scurrilous rhymes about his friends and enemies; these are dotted throughout his correspondence. For instance, he vented his spleen against Sir Horace Rumbold (whom he called Sir Whorearse Rumhole) not only by making him write the illiterate hangman's letter in *Ulysses* (p. 301) but in the following parody of Browning's 'Pippa Passes':

> *The Right Man in the Wrong Place*
>
> The pig's in the barley,
> The fat's in the fire:
> Old Europe can hardly
> Find twopence to buy her.
> Jack Spratt's in his office,
> Puffed, powdered and curled:
> Rumbold's in Warsaw—
> All's right with the world.

Two longer and meatier satirical poems than such squibs as this are printed as a makeweight in the present Faber edition of *Pomes Penyeach*. They are 'The Holy Office' of 1904, and 'Gas from a Burner' of 1912. These are probably his best poems; they are lively, witty and well-managed attacks on people who had annoyed or injured him.

The title of 'The Holy Office' betrays Joyce's anti-clericalism, but the poem's target is the 'mumming company' of Irish writers who were engaged in a resurgence of drama, poetry and novels in the Dublin that he was resolved to leave. According to him, they indulged in 'dreamy dreams'—which is a reference not only to the twilit Celtic legends that Yeats immersed himself in, but also to Yeats's mystical interests (as expounded in *A Vision*) and George Russell (A.E.)'s theosophy. Joyce attacked them for ignoring the physical side of life and, like his own Gerty MacDowell (his Nausicaa in *Ulysses*, Chapter XIII), thinking only in romantic and spiritual terms:

> 'But all these men of whom I speak
> Make me the sewer of their clique.
> That they may dream their dreamy dreams
> I carry off their filthy streams ...
> Thus I relieve their timid arses,
> Perform my office of Katharsis.'

(Of course, this is the 'holy office' that he means in the title. And the purging (Katharsis) is performed in a domestic office furnished with a hole.)

[Whatever truth there may have been in Joyce's ascription of spiritual bloodlessness to the poems of the early Yeats—such as 'The Lake Isle of Innisfree' or 'Had I the heaven's embroidered cloths'—it must be remembered that the later Yeats brought the physical side of love fully into consciousness in such lines as

> '... Love has pitched his mansion in
> The place of excrement.'   CRAZY JANE TALKS WITH THE BISHOP]

Secondly, and probably more bitingly, he regarded their whole woolly philosophy as soft-centred, lacking in intellectual rigour. They shamble, crouch, crawl and pray, whereas he stands erect, boldly challenging all comers like a stag on a mountain-ridge; they have

> '... souls that hate the strength that mine has
> Steeled in the school of old Aquinas.'

This mixture of Byronic self-doomed pride, mark of all romantic Cains, and intellectual arrogance, is one of the dominant features of Joyce's character. The last two lines:

> 'And though they spurn me from their door
> My soul shall spurn them evermore,'

which were written in the heat of the very moment when he was leaving Ireland, make an interesting contrast with the calmer rationalisation that he expressed when he looked back on Stephen Dedalus ten years later:

> 'I go to . . . forge in the smithy of my soul, the uncreated conscience of my race.'
>
> A PORTRAIT, p. 253

'Gas From a Burner' he wrote in a rage when the publisher who had signed a contract to publish *Dubliners* seemed finally to refuse to do so (see p. 18). It is a very funny but not greatly significant poem. It is written in the first person, as if by Roberts the publisher, who boasts of how broadminded he really is, having published many *avant-garde* works; but he cannot allow Joyce—

> 'that bloody fellow,
> That was over here dressed in Austrian yellow'—

to bring into disrepute the name of Ireland,

> 'This lovely land that always sent
> Her writers and artists to banishment,
> And in a spirit of Irish fun
> Betrayed her own leaders, one by one.'

The end is masterly. Roberts says:

> 'I'll burn that book, so help me devil . . .
> The very next Lent I will unbare
> My penitent buttocks to the air
> And sobbing beside my printing press
> My awful sin I will confess.
> My Irish foreman from Bannockburn
> Shall dip his right hand in the urn
> And sign crisscross with reverent thumb
> *Memento homo* upon my bum.'

This is not the James Joyce of his serious poems, collected in *Chamber Music* (1907) and *Pomes Penyeach* (1927). The only feature the scurrilous poems share with these is the technical excellence of the verse. The lyrics seem to come from a com-

pletely different pen, the pen which wrote the precious pale
effusion that Stephen Dedalus composed in *A Portrait*, p. 223.
This is a vilanelle, an example of a form which requires great
dexterity to manage its two rhymes and two alternating
refrains:

> Are you not weary of ardent ways,
> Lure of the fallen seraphim?
> Tell no more of enchanted days.

The obvious characteristics of this poem are its abundance of
highly-coloured incense-laden words such as seraphim, eucharis-
tic, and chalice; and a concentration on liquid phrases of small
significance: 'languorous look and lavish limb', for instance.

Of course one can dismiss this technically accomplished poem
as a prentice effort, and say that Joyce is looking mockingly if
still affectionately at the callow youth who produced it. But
Chamber Music abounds with lights of amethyst, night wind
answering in antiphon, revery, sweet bosom, light attire, virginal mien, welladay, zone, snood, cherubim, ancient plenilune,
epithalamium, grey and golden gossamer, soft tumult of thy
hair, tremulous, divers treasures, witchery, soft choiring of
delight, the waters' monotone. Well, you might argue that
Chamber Music dates from the same period of Joyce's development as *A Portrait*, so is bound to share its poetical style. But
Pomes Penyeach, put out by Joyce in his full maturity six years
after *Ulysses* was finished, abounds equally in love-blown ban-
nerets, shy sweet lures (see the vilanelle of Stephen), moondew,
lambent waters, thurible, laburnum tendrils and seraphim. Joyce
therefore conceived of his poems as musical noises interpreting
moods; the man who wrote the Verlainesque lines:

> All day I hear the noise of waters
>   Making moan
> Sad as the seabird is when going
>   Forth alone
> He hears the winds cry to the waters'
>   Monotone.   CHAMBER MUSIC XXXV

is the composer of the miraculous 'Sirens' chapter (XI) of *Ulysses*.

But he is also the mocking concocter of the romantic sugariness that opens the 'Nausicaa' chapter (XIII) in the words of Gerty MacDowell, devotee of women's trashy magazines (see p. 105). There is thus a paradox. Joyce wrote these swooning lyrics, expended much time and artistry on perfecting them, launched them into a cold world with every appearance of satisfaction; at the same time he denigrated their style and manner by calling one little book *Chamber Music*, which could be and indeed was a reference to the sound of water falling into a bedroom utensil, and the other *Pomes Penyeach*, a possibly mock-modest assertion that they were not worth very much— and he even offered a 'tilly', a little extra one, to give the customer thirteen, a baker's dozen, for the demanded shilling, or twelve pence of the purchase price.

The plain fact is that by our tastes today, in the post-Pound-and-Eliot era, these poems are empty exercises in factitious emotion-mongering. They are as soft-centred as anything written by the 'decadent' nineties poets or the Georgians, with their ripe sentiment, their hazy imagery and hazy rhythms, and their reliance on the mesmerising power of 'poetical' words:

> Meadows of England, shining in the rain,
> Spread wide your daisied lawns . . .
>
> Rupert Brooke, BRUMANA

or

> Let me go forth, and share
>   The overflowing Sun
>   With one wise friend, or one
> Better than wise, being fair . . .
>
> William Watson, ODE TO MAY

It was Ezra Pound who made the youthful T. S. Eliot focus his images precisely, and so changed the course of English poetry:

46

Remark the cat which flattens itself in the gutter,
Slips out its tongue
And devours a morsel of rancid butter

T. S. Eliot, RHAPSODY ON A WINDY NIGHT

And oddly enough it was Ezra Pound who 'discovered' James Joyce through reading the last poem of *Chamber Music*, 'I hear an Army charging upon the land'. This poem does present a hard violent image, and could well at first be taken as an Imagist poem, like those of Wyndham Lewis or Richard Aldington, who were heading the new movement; then in the last two lines it tries to tie the image to the mood of the despairing love-lorn poet. It is, however, very different from the others in the book, which all seem to lack energy. If Joyce was to be a leader of any literary revolution, it was clearly not to be through his lyrical poems. As Anthony Powell says (in *Encounter*, February 1973), talking of Picasso:

> One cannot help wondering whether violent experiment was not vital for Picasso, to avoid becoming trapped in personal emotions less profound than his actual skill as a painter. A parallel might possibly be drawn with Joyce, fleeing from his earlier naturalism, in order to save himself from the artificiality and elaboration of the late 19th century. This may be seen in *A Portrait of the Artist as a Young Man* where . . . occur pomposities of phrasing that nothing short of *Ulysses* would cure. In somewhat the same manner did Picasso turn to Cubism, Africa, and all the experiments that followed, to control an innate sentimentality and romanticism.

Joyce did indeed use his poems as an escape from the literalism of his meticulously detailed and precisely accurate exposition of the ordinary; in them he records his yearnings and his transient states of feeling. They are mood music.

If *Chamber Music* is read continuously from the beginning, a sequence of moods can be felt. Rather like some romantic cycles of songs (Schumann's *Frauenliebe und Leben* or Tennyson's *Maud*, for example), they pass from early love, possibly through marriage or consummation, to desertion and despair. The story is not explicitly told; each poem can be read as a separate expression of emotion. Their outstanding virtue is the extreme delicacy of the verse. The words are chosen for their subtle sound, and there are close associations with the scriptures, especially the Song of Solomon, and with Shakespeare and the English madrigalists, as well as with contemporary poetical swoony language.

Pomes Penyeach do not make up a whole. They are short lyrics, very like the earlier poems in style and content, but they appear to be celebrating events, significant moments or moods in Joyce's life. 'She weeps over Rahoon', for example, is about Nora Joyce's first lover who had died young (see p. 23 for fuller explanation). Another talks of a flower given to his daughter Lucia, and seems with hindsight to foreshadow the mental and spiritual troubles that were to beset her (see p. 17). 'On the Beach at Fontana' enshrines a moment of loving fear for his son Giorgio. Others refer to nothing indentifiable; but all are short and poignant in expression, and clearly meant much to the poet, even if they communicate little to us beyond a vague gush of feeling encapsulated in an image that relies rather on sound than sense. One short lyric printed in the present Faber edition is supernumerary to the original baker's dozen: it tells of the near coincidence of the death of Joyce's father with the birth of his grandson, and ends with a prayer for his father's forgiveness—probably for deserting Ireland and for not offering the willing financial support that his father had hoped James's brilliant career as a doctor or professor would provide.

> A child is sleeping:
> An old man gone.
> O, father forsaken,
> Forgive your son!   ECCE PUER

Coincidentally, the best poem—at least the hardest and most vital—among the thirteen in *Pomes Penyeach* is the 'tilly' that begins the collection, which refers to the death many years before of his mother.

6

Ulysses

The first thing to note on attacking *Ulysses* is the overall plan of the book.

You can, of course, embark on *Ulysses* in the ordinary way: just begin at the beginning and read on. But you will soon come up against obstacles of meaning and organisation that will make it all but impossible to go on. My own experience, at any rate, was that I tried twice to read it, and on each occasion reached only a point about a third of the way through. Until I was asked to teach Joyce I never found the time or the mental discipline necessary to read it; but now that I have done so, or possibly because I have done so, I am convinced that it is the most complete work of art of this century. It is well worth walking all the way round it before examining the details. Indeed, the details take on their proper significance only when the total intention, as embodied in the plan, is understood.

The 700 pages are divided into eighteen chapters, each of which is placed temporally in one of the twenty-four hours of a specific day. Chapter I begins at eight o'clock in the morning of 16 June 1904, and Chapter XVIII ends at about three o'clock in the early hours of 17 June. Each chapter visits a different place, but the Unity of Place is observed as well as the Unity of Time, for all the places are in or near Dublin: the first is an old tower—one of the Martello towers, erected along the coast of the United Kingdom as a defence against Napoleon Bonaparte; and the last is the matrimonial bed of Mr. and Mrs. Leopold Bloom in Number 7 Eccles Street; the places of all the intervening chapters add up to a general topographical presentation of the city of Dublin. Each chapter was originally headed by Joyce with a Homeric title drawn from the *Odyssey*; Telemachus, Ulysses' son, opens the story, and Penelope, his wife, closes it. Some people think it is a pity that Joyce decided to remove these titles in the final printing; one can only surmise that, having used them as a stimulus and a guide to composition, he felt they would be a distracting influence on the reader—just as a musical expounder's voice calling out 'First Subject', 'Second Subject', is a distraction to listeners to a Haydn Symphony, once they have learnt to recognise the shape of a sonata form first movement for themselves.

So far, these formal props to the work are not particularly recondite. But Joyce, in his totally committed labyrinthine way, also organised the book round various organs of the body, various arts and sciences, departments of human knowledge, and various recurring or dominant symbols. Thus in Chapter IV the Kidney is prominent, in Chapter VII the Lungs, and in Chapter XIV the Womb. Chapters I, II and III have no specific physical organ because they are preoccupied with the mind, not the body, of the intellectual Stephen Dedalus, rather than the *homme moyen sensuel*, Leopold Bloom. Chapter I, again, has many references to theology, whereas Chapter IX, in which prominent members of the Irish literary movement debate about Shakespeare in a library, celebrates Literature. As for the symbols, these recur in a complex pattern which permeates the book, but certain ones are more prominent in certain chapters— Barmaids in Chapter XI, for instance, and Mothers in Chapter XIV.

But Joyce was not only composing to an elaborate plan, of which the salient features are set out in the foregoing paragraphs. More upsettingly to the innocent reader, he varied his style, or rather, as he called it, his *method*, in each of the eighteen chapters. This is at first sight the most difficult feature of the book, and probably is responsible for discouraging more readers than all the other peculiarities.

For example, the famous last chapter, Molly Bloom's interior soliloquy of forty-six pages without any punctuation at all, is characterised as *monologue* (*female*); the 'Sirens', Chapter XI, where the ear is the organ and music the art, imitates a *fuga per canonem* (naturally not very closely, since a medium employing words is so very different from one employing notes); and the chapter on the Cyclops, Chapter XII, frequently bursts out in huge extravaganzas in which one idea is developed to an extremely disproportionate degree: Joyce called this *gigantism*.

This series of devices makes for variety, but it adds enormously to the complexity of the work, and must have caused Joyce immense trouble as well as intense delight in the writing. To Joyce, words were entirely subservient, as they were to Humpty-Dumpty in *Alice Through the Looking-glass*. He ordered them to do what he wanted them to, and if the result, like Humpty-Dumpty's, is *impenetrability*, well, his readers must find the key and learn how to apply it.

For the form of any work is not merely an arbitrary shape imposed on its ideas for the sake of convenience. It is an integral and essential factor in its total effect; the fourteen-line shape of the sonnet is part of its meaning. When you read a well-wrought sonnet you feel that everything has been said, and in an unalterable manner. So with *Ulysses*; its form is an inalienable part of it, and it is unthinkable in any other.

Having looked at the plan (though it will be referred to again and again as we look at individual chapters), let us now look at the content of the book. What is it about?

There are three main characters: Stephen Dedalus, hero of *A Portrait of the Artist as a Young Man*, Leopold Bloom, aged thirty-eight, an Irish-born Jew of Hungarian extraction, and his unfaithful wife Marion or Molly Bloom, who is something of a singer. In the first three chapters we are admitted into the mind of Stephen; he has just returned from the self-imposed exile that concluded *A Portrait* to attend his mother's deathbed, and is now very much at a loose end in Dublin; his home has almost broken up, his temporary teaching job does not satisfy him, and he feels his undoubted talents are wasted in a city which does not recognise his genius. He is seen in many situations during the day, but after 'his' chapters the interest is focused on Bloom. This kindly, ineffective, unsuccessful fringe member of the business world begins his day by taking Molly's breakfast to her in bed; he goes out on his peripatetic freelance job of collecting advertisements for a local newspaper, a job which involves his meeting all sorts of people in all sorts of places, and as he wanders about Dublin contact is made not only with this busy provincial capital but also with a couple of hundred people, who are encountered as they meet and part, talk and sing and act. More important, perhaps, the reader gets to know Bloom as no other character in fiction. After the 'Stephen' chapters, all but two are centred on Bloom and take place largely in his mind or in his presence. His preoccupations with his job, his wife and her lover Blazes Boylan, his futile and silly flirtation with a typist he has never met, his philosophical speculations and sexual phantasies, his living daughter and dead son, and increasingly as the book proceeds his fatherly interest in Stephen—all these gradually build up an intimate picture of an ostensibly, even ostentatiously, ordinary man: at the same time the city of Dublin and the lives and preoccupations of its inhabitants are similarly made known. Joyce himself said to Frank Budgen, 'I want to give a picture of Dublin so complete that if the city one day suddenly disappeared from the earth it could be reconstructed out of my book.'

The central Chapter X in particular, 'The Wandering Rocks', dodges about the city in nineteen interlinked episodes, in which nearly all the characters in the book meet and pass or just fail to meet, as in daily life. This is one of the two chapters, after the first three 'Stephen' chapters, not specifically based on Bloom, but his presence is still there; the other is the final one, 'Penelope', forty-six pages of Molly Bloom's thoughts as she lies in bed after a day in which she has been technically unfaithful to her husband. But this chapter too cannot distract us from Bloom for long, because Molly's thoughts are never far away from him.

Stephen, Bloom, Molly, Dublin: are these all that the book is about? No. Most important also are the techniques or methods which Joyce employs; as was said a couple of pages back, the form is part of the meaning, and it cannot be separated from the book's content. In portraying the thoughts of one Bloom, his wife and his new-found surrogate 'son' on one day in one city, Joyce is also presenting a universalised picture of the human condition. It is a commonplace nowadays to declare that in Hamlet or Dorothea Brooke or Oedipus or Gregers we see ourselves; by revealing their intensely individual minds in reaction to their immensely different spatial or temporal environments their creators are showing us how they themselves tick, and also how we tick. That is, it seems to me, what art is about. Who can look at Rembrandt's portrait of his aged mother reading (in Wilton House, near Salisbury) without feeling that all human joys and sorrows are recorded on that half a square yard of canvas? Who can hear the 'Egmont' Overture without also feeling Beethoven's unconquerable aspiration to freedom for himself and for all mankind almost as explicit as in the great Freedom Chorus from *Fidelio*? Yet without the technical dexterity of the artist and composer these would have been lost; ordinary men would have known less about old Vrouw Rembrandt and less about Beethoven; but also less about themselves. And they are none the less works of art, examples of their own medium, constructed and executed according to the logical process of their own art. Rembrandt was a painter, Beethoven a musician; they were not philosophers.

Joyce, in choosing his own form, which evolved slowly and painfully over seven or eight years of constant meditation and experiment, was trying to depict not only the human mind, but the human body without which the mind cannot exist, at least to temporal knowledge—hence the fifteen 'organs' of Chapters IV to XVIII. 'In my book', said Joyce to Budgen, 'the body lives in and moves through space and is the home of a full human personality.' So with the seventeen 'arts and sciences', so with the inter-related symbols and cross-references. Human life is a complex amalgam, and in the attempt to represent in an intelligible form the chaos of it—thoughts, impressions, feelings, physical sensations, evanescent intimations as if from other worlds—only a complex yet seemingly haphazard pattern can do it justice. Thus *Ulysses* is so constructed that we can only understand it when we have finished it; and we then need to go back to the beginning and read it again with full knowledge of its ending.

It may well be thought that a book which must be read once through before it is comprehended, before even the significance of its parts is realised, is an oddity that demands too much. But *Ulysses* is not by any means unique in this respect. It may be amusing to guess what famous English novel is being referred to in the following passage:

> For this is not an easy book to read; it should never be the beginner's primer, nor be published without a prefatory synopsis. Only when the story has been thoroughly assimilated, can the infinite delights and subtleties of its workmanship be appreciated, as you realise the manifold complexity of the book's web, and find that every sentence, almost every epithet, has its definite reference to equally unemphasised points before and after in the development of the plot. Thus it is that, while twelve readings of *Pride and Prejudice* give you twelve periods of pleasure repeated, as many readings of   give you that pleasure, not repeated only, but squared and squared again with each perusal, till at every fresh reading you feel anew that you never understood anything like the widening sum of its delights. But, until you know the story, you are apt to find its movement dense and slow and obscure, difficult to follow, and not very obviously worth the following.

Apart from the reference to a 'story', which in the accepted sense of the term can hardly apply to it, these words could be a description of *Ulysses*. But they were written of *Emma*, on the occasion of the centenary of Jane Austen's death in 1917, while *Ulysses* was being composed.

But in fact this book, like life, has no ending, as it has no beginning.

Many novels begin and end with the hero's birth and death, and many more begin with the meeting of the hero and heroine and end in their marriage; even Joyce's *Portrait* begins with 'baby tuckoo' and ends with Stephen's definite act of self-exile; but any hero is only one individual in a vast crowd of family, friends and acquaintances, and the relationships can obviously be made to stretch ever more widely, as ripples spread out from the dropped stone in a pond; the novelist has to give his pond, however large, shores beyond which the ripples cannot extend. Thus a novel is a pond, while life is a sea without shores. Another author, who seems to be as different from Joyce as Jane Austen was, has posed the problem in these words:

> Really, universally, relations stop nowhere, and the exquisite problem of the artist is eternally but to draw, by a geometry of his own, the circle within which they shall happily *appear* to do so. He is in the perpetual predicament that the continuity of things is the whole matter, for him, of comedy and tragedy; that this continuity is never, by the space of an instant or an inch, broken, and that, to do anything at all, he has at once intensely to consult and intensely to ignore it.   Henry James: Preface TO RODERICK HUDSON

In *Ulysses*, Joyce makes hardly any progress with a 'story'; he ignores such concepts as comedy and tragedy, which require a plot of causal relations; and the teeming inconsequential continuity of life in Dublin, on a specific day in 1904, is glimpsed as it was experienced in the minds of his three chief personages, but mainly through the eyes of Bloom, his very ordinary non-hero. Any twenty-four hours in any one of the thousands of days of the civilised life of mankind would have served as material for Joyce's task; but to the individual writer James Joyce, only 16 June 1904 would suffice at the moment when he was writing; and he chose this day because this was the very day when his relationship with Nora, his wife-to-be, began.

The solution of the enigma of form, then, is necessary to our understanding of the book. But it would be idle to presume that a mere reader can appreciate everything that the artist, the maker, the poet, did. The ordinary person who can hardly write a good sentence cannot possibly understand more than a fraction of the considerations which weighed with Joyce as he worked. A passage in Mozart's letters may be used to point the inevitable ignorance of the listener. He is talking about composing his opera, *Il Seraglio*, and the problem of depicting the ridiculous rage of the harem-keeper Osmin when he finds someone trying to get in; the reader can see and understand some of the things that Mozart does: the quicker notes, then the quicker tempo are fairly obvious, and as we listen to the music we could notice these for ourselves. He would even probably notice a change of key; but unless he is a musical scholar he would not recognise the key to which Osmin changes, and even if he did we would not see that 'the further A minor' was chosen in preference to 'the nearest D minor' exactly because Mozart wanted Osmin's overstepping of all moderation to be epitomised in the key relationships. And over all this there remains, constant and omnipotent, the principle that 'music even in the most aweful places must not offend the ear, but give pleasure'; while the whole conception of the magnificent aria is tied explicitly to the voice of a particular singer at a specific opera-house on a specific day 200 years ago. Had this man's voice not ranged so far and so expressively, *Il Seraglio* would have been a different opera.

Here is the passage:

> The rage of Osmin will be rendered comic: in the execution of the aria I have let his fine deep voice display itself. The 'Drum beym Barte des Propheten' is actually in the same tempo but with quicker notes, and as his rage increases then—when one thinks the aria is at an end—the *allegro assai* in quite another tempo and in another key must make a splendid effect; for a man who is in such a rage oversteps all moderation, measure and bounds; he does not know himself—so the music must not; although the utmost passion, violent or not, must never be pushed as far as the disgusting, and music even in the most aweful places must not offend the ear, but give pleasure; that is, music must always remain music; so I have chosen no foreign key to the F [key of the aria] but a consonant one; not, however, the nearest D minor but the further A minor.

Joyce had a mind just as subtle and just as obsessed with creation as Mozart's. Frank Budgen tells the story of how Joyce said he had worked for a whole day on two sentences, seeking the perfect order of already chosen words so as to create the effect of a man at once hungry for his lunch and obsessively engaged with silk underclothes in a shop window.

> Perfume of embraces all him assailed. With hungered flesh
> obscurely, he mutely craved to adore.   p. 168

You and I would have been satisfied with any one of a dozen different word-orders; we cannot see how there can be only one perfect order, and so we can only dimly perceive how Joyce spent his day. We may even suspect that Joyce was having a little quiet fun at the expense of his credulous friend. But bearing in mind the Mozart passage, I do not think so. Only Joyce himself knew what was the right order, and only he could find it by obeying his own sense of what he wanted to say.

But even if we cannot follow all the ramifications of the creative process, the more we know of it, the more we haltingly explore it, the deeper will be our understanding of the work. And in the case of *Ulysses* it is essential to penetrate some distance into the mind of its creator. When we know that he spent a whole working day on two lines, it is no longer surprising that the 700 pages occupied him for seven years or more—an average speed of about one page every three and a half days!

Joyce's method of composition, in the later stages especially, was most complicated. He wanted the wholeness of the book to be apparent, and to this end, as the writing proceeded, he built up a store of notes of phrases, incidents, names of people and things which he then, in the final stages, inserted into the earlier chapters. At the end, he had a whole valise full of notes, which by employing a system of coloured pencils he assigned to various episodes; since some of the earlier episodes had already been printed, it was more difficult to insert the references into their text, and the style of these is usually less complicated. However, this did not deter Joyce from making alterations (see illustrations) right up to the last possible moment in the proof-correcting. His printers must often have been in despair when they saw their carefully printed proofs criss-crossed and interlined with new material; and the extra cost must have been colossal. Again it is apparent how Joyce's single-minded view of the over-riding importance of his work put everyone else, and of course himself, to endless trouble.

So as the writing proceeded over the seven long years from 1914 to 1921, and beyond that in the proof stage, Joyce built up a list of additions and revisions that had to be inserted into all the episodes, both those already written and those still to come. Thus you cannot truly appreciate the wholeness of the design of the book until you have come to the end of it. But once you have taken in all the multifarious themes, the details of cross-reference, the repeated symbols, and the events constantly referred to (which can only be fully done when you have finished it) you will have in your mind something approaching the complete, grand, all-inclusive image of human life that Joyce strove so long and so ardently to capture. The result is extra-ordinarily exciting; but you have to work for it, and work pretty hard.

One intriguing question remains to be discussed: to what extent is it necessary for the reader to know about the Homeric parallels, the most obvious of which is the title?

My own view is that you should have read the *Odyssey* in a good plain prose translation. This is not because the correspon-dence between Homer and Joyce is always very close. In 'The Lestrygonians', for instance, all that it is necessary to know is that these fierce people were cannibals; Joyce merely describes in Chapter VIII how Bloom was momentarily disgusted at the spectacle of men in a crowded smelly restaurant chewing away at their steaks and chops, spitting out bits of half-masticated gristle and speaking with their mouths full (p. 169). 'The Wandering Rocks', Chapter X, has reference only to one line in the *Odyssey*, where the voyage of the Argonauts, another story altogether, is mentioned; Odysseus did not himself have to navigate this particular peril. No one has, as far as I know, yet made out a good case for a 'Scylla and Charybdis' parallel in Chapter IX; there are various conflicting guesses. But sometimes it is a great help to know, even if only dimly, what was in Joyce's mind as he constructed an episode. The first six books of the *Odyssey* are called 'the Telemachia', because in them

Telemachus, Odysseus' son, depressed and frustrated by the ten-year-long occupation of his mother's palace by usurping suitors, sets out on a voyage to find his father; and the first three chapters of *Ulysses* tell of the frustration of Stephen, of his giving up the key of the tower he rented to the 'usurper', Buck Mulligan, as he sets out on his voyage across Dublin, which culminates in his meeting with Odysseus-Bloom and their establishing a rapport that gives a promise to both their futures.

To the writer of the book, however, the *Odyssey* was the constant underlying framework to which he could come back for the necessary control of the vast mass of material to which he was always adding. We know that Joyce had been obsessed with the Odysseus story from early childhood. It had reverberated in his mind, and the project that finally took the form that we know went through many stages of development. He came to see Odysseus as the representative of all mankind, more completely typical than any other character in history or mythology. An illuminating reference to Odysseus, that Joyce must have read, comes in Plato's *Republic*. In that part of Book X which treats of 'The Immortality of the Soul', Plato describes how the souls of dead people chose by lot the lives they will live in their next incarnation. Different types of life were set before them—successful or unsuccessful tyranny, high birth, athletic fame—and having drawn lots for the order of choice, the souls chose according to their wisdom and experience of their past lives.

> It was a sight worth seeing, all those souls choosing lives for themselves. It was pitiful, laughable, amazing! Most of them chose something like their former lives. I saw the soul that had once belonged to Orpheus choosing the life of a swan because he didn't want to be given birth by a woman; women had caused his death and he hated them all. I saw the soul of Thamyris choosing the life of a nightingale; and a swan and other singing birds deciding to change into human beings. The twentieth soul on the list chose the life of a lion; this was Telamonian Ajax, who remembered the Award of Arms and rejected human shape. The one after this was

Agamemnon; his sufferings had made him a hater of men as well, and he decided to turn into an eagle. Half-way down the list came the soul of Atalanta, who chose the life of an athlete; she saw the great honours it offered, and couldn't resist it. . . . Near the end of the line was Thersites the clown taking on the form of a monkey. And last of all, as it happened, was Odysseus. After his earlier troubles he had had enough of the rat-race, and spent a long time looking around for the life of a simple nonentity. At last he found one; the others had passed it by, but when he saw it he took it delightedly, saying that it was just what he would have chosen if he had had first pick.   Plato: THE REPUBLIC. Book X § 620
translated by James Sabben-Clare

Whether Joyce picked up this reference or not, it is so apposite that it could almost be a description of *Ulysses*—a day in the uneventful life of an ordinary man. For Joyce is at pains not only to make Bloom as ordinary as possible, without intellectual brilliance or charisma, but also to make us feel that such ordinary men as he have been living ordinary lives, yet not devoid of heroism in their small circles, ever since civilisation began.

The Homeric parallels, therefore, are significant to Joyce, and useful to ordinary readers. But, as was suggested earlier (p. 50), it is better that they should remain in the background as attention is concentrated on the event of Bloomsday, 16 June 1904.

It is now time to look more closely at the text. What follows is a summary of the events and a commentary on those features of the successive chapters which it is necessary, in my view, to master on a first reading. Before embarking on each section, you should read the relevant chapter as quickly as you can, so as to get the flavour of it. (References are to the Penguin text of *Ulysses*, first published 1969.) You can then go over it more slowly with the help of this, necessarily selective, guide. As you progress, Joyce's method will begin to speak for itself, and those features that are common to the chapters will stand out more clearly as the grand design of the book emerges.

It appears that Joyce did not want his various frameworks for the book (the *Odyssey*, the body, the arts, the techniques, etc.) to be explicit. Hence the deletion of the Homeric titles, which he had used, if only for convenience of reference, in the construction of the grand edifice. But though he printed no guide to *Ulysses*, he sent private ones to various friends and encouraged his translator into French, Stuart Gilbert, in the compilation of his version of the total scheme, which is published in Gilbert's book *James Joyce's Ulysses*; this is regarded as a fairly accurate interpretation of Joyce's intentions.

There are other schemes, such as that which Joyce sent to Carlo Linati in 1920. An interesting comparison of the Gilbert and Linati versions, which differ in many details but not in total import, can be found in Richard Ellmann's recent book, *Ulysses on the Liffey* (1972). The fact that the two schemes differ tends to demonstrate that Joyce did not set much store by the details, many of which appear to be fortuitous. Indeed, he once confessed to Samuel Beckett that he felt he had over-systematised *Ulysses*.

Richard Ellmann's book explores the possibility of another scheme in Joyce's mind, a more philosophical one than either Gilbert's or Linati's. He divides *Ulysses* into six groups of three chapters, or triads, each with a sequence of thesis, antithesis and synthesis. The ingenuity with which the philosophical propositions are discovered, and the wit of the writing, make this book a pleasure to read and a source of new enlightenment. It does not invalidate the earlier schemes, but opens up fresh avenues for the exploration of Joyce's thought and method.

The present short study is based on the Gilbert scheme, which is readily available. As has been pointed out, however, the reader should not regard this scheme, or Linati's, or any other he might come across, as definitive, but use it only as a general guide to Joyce's intentions. The creative spirit could not suffer to be bound by any such rigid formulation.

CHAPTER I

Homeric parallel: Telemachus.   Art: Theology.
Time: 8 a.m.   Place: The Martello Tower.
Technique: Narrative (young).   Symbol: Heir.

Stephen Dedalus is the subject of *A Portrait of the Artist as a Young Man*, so the reader knows him well enough not to need much introduction. In fact, these first pages were originally planned as part of *A Portrait*. There is therefore no break between the two books, which helps to explain why the story begins without preamble; but there are mystifications right from the start, and we must be wide awake to catch the implications of what we read, so as to mould them into a composite whole as they unfold, referring backwards and forwards. For instance, in *A Portrait* Stephen has become a lapsed Catholic and a failed priest; so when Buck Mulligan enters 'stately' in the very first word, bearing a bowl with crossed implements on it, intoning Latin church ritual, he is clearly pulling Stephen's leg. He calls to someone named Kinch, 'a fearful jesuit'; but we don't know for certain that Stephen is Kinch until ten lines later, or what Kinch means until the next page. Nor does Joyce give us any set description of the place; we must pick up 'stairhead', 'mild morning air', 'round gunrest', 'tower', surrounding country, awaking mountains, parapet; we don't know it's a Martello tower until p. 24. We learn that Stephen pays the rent, £12 for an unspecified time, that Mulligan has brought there an Oxford student called Haines, whom Stephen hates as a representative of the oppressing British: there is an echo of the dialogue with another affected Englishman, the Dean of Studies in *A Portrait*, and his condescending folklorish interest in the word 'tundish' that so offended Stephen. (*Tundish* was apparently a normal word for a funnel—for filling bottles, barrels or *tuns*—in Ireland, but it also occurs in Shakespeare.) There is no explanation of what is happening, no filling in of the background. It is all taken for granted as in everyday life. Stephen knew who Buck Mulligan was, knew about his rich aunt and his drinking habits and his cynical views of religion and his inexhaustible fund of bawdy songs, stories and catchphrases; he did not need to be told. So we too must absorb the circumstances as we go along, gradually accumulating facts and atmosphere together.

It is not quite accurate to say that this chapter is in narrative form. True, the events, remarks, actions of the three young men during the hour beginning at eight o'clock are told in sequence as they happened. But mixed up with these are the thoughts in Stephen's mind, so that quick shifts from what might be called the author's viewpoint to Stephen's viewpoint often occur. For instance, on p. 17, from line 3:

> Dedalus, come down, like a good mosey. Breakfast is ready. Haines is apologising for waking us last night . . . ,

the words and actions of Mulligan and Stephen are narrated in a normal way, finishing with a snatch of a pub song:

> O, *won't we have a merry time*
>   *On coronation day?*

Without warning, at this point there is a flash for three lines into Stephen's mind:

> Warm sunshine merrying over the sea. The nickel shavingbowl shone, forgotten, on the parapet. Why should I bring it down? Or leave it there all day, forgotten friendship.

This captures magically the impressions and feelings of Stephen's mind—the sensation of sunlight and the view of the sea, entwined with the *merry* of the song Mulligan is even then singing as he descends the stairs; the shavingbowl out of its place, and Stephen's slight resentment at Mulligan's carelessness, and his lordly assumption that someone else will clear up after him; the impending break with Mulligan, whose friendship Stephen is even then beginning to reject.

The next four lines are a mixture of narrative and thought:

> He went over to it, held it in his hands awhile, feeling its coolness, smelling the clammy slaver of the lather in which the brush was stuck. So I carried the boat of incense at Clongowes. I am another now and yet the same. A servant too. A server of a servant.

Here the first sentence begins with a normal external narrative, but soon switches to Stephen's sensations, of touch, smell and sight combined. Then without warning 'He' changes to 'I', and we are in Stephen's memory of Clongowes Academy, the school Stephen attended in *A Portrait*.

Then until p. 20, l. 8:

> He watched her pour into the measure and thence into the jug rich white milk, not hers. Old shrunken paps,

occur two pages of uninterrupted external narrative. During these two pages several things emerge: that Stephen has just been to Paris, that Haines is collecting folklore, that Stephen and Mulligan enjoy pulling Haines's leg, that an old peasant woman brings them the milk.

In this confusing manner we gradually become aware of the prickly personality of Stephen: 'an impossible person', Mulligan calls him. But we also gain respect for his quick-ranging mind, erudite and witty. Naturally, there are references that cannot easily be picked up; as with any other author's work, recourse must be had to the notes unless the reader has the same mental furniture as the author. A full set of even brief notes on *Ulysses* would need to be as long as the text, as in modern editions of Shakespeare. Into this comparatively simple chapter, for example, intrude Chrysostomos, p. 9, the Mabinogion and the Upanishads, p. 19, and a whole list of heretical Church Fathers on p. 27. I do not think it worth the effort on a first study of the book, however, to track all these down in the Encyclopaedias, even though it is necessary to full understanding. I suggest that you pick up what references you can and ignore the rest until you come to study specially attractive sections of the book at greater leisure. Otherwise you will never get to the end, and as I have already said, it is essential that you do.

Joyce's system of cross-references is already in operation in this chapter; remarks which seem quite casual are later found to have been quite significant. For instance, on p. 28 a young man clinging to a spur of rock in the water casually gossips with Mulligan just before he plunges in. Mention is made of the Bannon family in Westmeath, with whom Mulligan's brother is staying, and we hear that Bannon has found a 'sweet young thing down there. Photo girl he calls her.' Later on it is revealed that this is Bloom's daughter Milly, whose letter to her father (p. 68) from the photographer's shop in Westmeath where she works mentions a young student named Bannon. Much later (p. 399) Mulligan and Bannon come together into the common room at the maternity hospital, where Bloom is drinking with the young doctors and medical students, and Bannon shows the company a photograph of Milly and declares how affecting she looked in her new 'coquette cap'. This was the Sterneian phrase for a tam-o'-shanter (a sort of Scottish beret) that Bloom had given her for her birthday present, and which is also mentioned as 'my new tam' in Milly's thank-you letter on p. 68. (The passage on p. 401 is written in the sort of prose Sterne had used in *A Sentimental Journey*.) Milly in her letter had declared that everyone said she was 'quite the belle' in her new hat, and Joyce picks up not only her own feelings about the hat but also her character as a flirtatious daughter of Molly Bloom, and translates all this into the arch tone of the philandering parson Sterne, encapsulated in the one word 'coquette'. What a brilliant writer he is!

More important themes are touched on in this first 'young narrative' chapter. Perhaps the most important is the theme of father and son (pp. 22 and 24); this is a foretaste of the Shakespeare and Hamlet discussion which occupies the central position in the 'Scylla and Charybdis' section, Chapter IX.

One feature of *Ulysses* is the recurrence not only of the major themes, such as Father and Son, but also of seemingly unimportant objects (for want of a better word) such as tea, key, cow, urine, hat, flower, pot, eucharist, stick. It is amusing to recognise these as they make their unifying contribution to the apparent chaos of impressions, thoughts and events. They are so many and so frequent that it is impossible to do more than notice a few, as they come, but those nine mentioned above are all in this chapter, with many more, and they will occur again, in perhaps more significant contexts.

Finally, this chapter has several beautifully concise thumbnail sketches. One of them is of a ragging and debagging of an undergraduate, probably in Oxford; this is on p. 13, and is well worth studying as an example of Joyce's command of his medium—words. The noisy roistering bullies with their 'moneyed voices' and their slangy catchphrases contrast tellingly with the old deaf gardener 'with Matthew Arnold's face' mowing the 'sombre' lawn in the quiet quadrangle below. Every word in these twelve lines has its point; but the oblique reference to 'new paganism' is a reminder of Arnold's indictment of the 'Philistines' in his Oxford lectures.

CHAPTER II

Homeric parallel: Nestor.   Art: History.
Time: 10 a.m.   Place: Mr. Deasy's School.
Technique: Catechism (personal).   Symbol: Horse.

This short chapter deals with Stephen's rejection of yet another bond with his time and place. He has been teaching for an unspecified but short time (probably three weeks) in a preparatory school for well-to-do boys, and is now about to give up this comparatively well-paid employment, in order to have freedom to follow his genius. Still weighing on his conscience is his rejection of his mother—on p. 34 there is another reference to the 'odour of wetted ashes' (pp. 11 and 43), associated with her deathbed—but now she has become part of history, part of his own history; and it is everything that history implies that he is trying to escape from. He wants to start afresh.

Thus it is doubly frustrating for him that he is now teaching

Greek history (what else?), and the chapter begins with his questions and the boys' answers in a history lesson. This is the *catechism, personal,* of the method for this chapter, or at least for the start of it. As is now expected, woven into the narrative of the lesson, into the catechism, are Stephen's own thoughts. It is the thoughts which are the more important. This leads inescapably to the conclusion that just as the Homeric parallels are only of limited importance, which in any case varies from chapter to chapter, so the scheme of techniques or methods is more of a prop to the writer than a directive to the reader. Indeed, one often feels that to some extent the scheme is imposed on the finished work by critics and analysts.

The Homeric parallel of Nestor is quite useful in this chapter. In the *Odyssey,* Telemachus seeks advice from the wise old King of Pylos, who is also a lover of horses. Clearly Mr. Deasy fulfils this role with Stephen; he gives him advice about paying his way and looking after his money; and his study is full of treasures—coins, shells, and pictures of horses. On pp. 37 to 39 there are half a dozen references to horses and horse-racing. But Mr. Deasy is also interested in foot-and-mouth disease in cattle; as Ireland lived largely by exporting dairy products, cattle and horses, the treatment of this disease by inoculation rather than its eradication by wholesale slaughter (still the British veterinary policy) was a matter of some moment, and Mr. Deasy writes (using his typewriter's *keys,* p. 38) a letter which he hopes Stephen can get into the Dublin press through his literary connections. Naturally more will be heard of this letter in later chapters; *cows,* already noted, are one of the recurring symbols. And not only is it later transferred into the newspaper columns (for example on pp. 395 and 568) but Stephen tears off the blank end of the second page to jot down a flash of inspiration (p. 53) and hands the mutilated letter to Myles Thomas, editor of the paper which published it (p. 133). References to foot-and-mouth disease are frequent in the book; and Stephen guesses (on p. 42) that as a consequence of his getting the letter published he will earn the epithet 'bullock-befriending bard' from Mulligan, which of course he does, and these words recur, too.

Another reference to notice is on p. 34, where Stephen, helping a dullard with his algebra, remembers Mulligan's joke on p. 24 about Stephen's ability to prove by algebra that Hamlet's grandson is Shakespeare's grandfather and that he himself is the ghost of his own father. Stephen will have more to say about Hamlet and Shakespeare in Chapter IX, but here the interesting thing is that Stephen feels again his inability to escape from his unsatisfactory self, built up as it is on the foundations of his own childhood. He sits beside the boy, working through his problems with him.

> Like him was I, these sloping shoulders, this gracelessness. My childhood bends beside me. Too far for me to lay a hand there once or lightly. Mine is far and his secret as our eyes. Secrets, silent, stony sit in the dark palaces of both our hearts: secrets weary of their tyranny: tyrants willing to be dethroned.   p. 34

And a little later, as Mr. Deasy pays him for the third time:

> The same room and hour, the same wisdom: and I the same. Three times now. Three nooses round me here. Well, I can break them in this instant if I will.   p. 36

Later still (p. 40):

> —History, Stephen said, is a nightmare from which I am trying to awake.

CHAPTER III

> Homeric parallel: Proteus.   Art: Philology.
> Time: 11 a.m.   Place: Sandymount Strand.
> Technique: Monologue (male).   Symbol: Tide.

The 'Telemachia', the first three chapters dealing with young Stephen as the first six of the *Odyssey* are about Telemachus, concludes with another short chapter, which is completely in interior monologue—Stephen's thoughts. Well, not quite absolutely completely, for an occasional sentence or phrase of narrative is necessary for clarity—e.g. 'Stephen closed his eyes,' 'His pace slackened.'

Stephen broods on his situation, on his family, his rejected religion, his unfulfilled ambitions as a writer, his experiences in Paris, Mulligan, Ireland and its rebel politicians, language, literature, and of course on the meaning of existence. The shifts in his thought are occasioned largely by what he sees and does as he walks along the sea-shore—two midwives with a bag (p. 43), the tide-mark of dried seaweed (p. 46), the sunlight on the sea-wall (p. 48), a dead and a live dog (p. 50), cocklepickers (p. 52), the incoming tide and the seaweed floating in it (p. 55), and finally a ship sailing into Dublin harbour (p. 56). As Stephen walks along the strand the surface of which changes from dry sand to sea-wrack to boulder-strewn beach, he listens to the sound of his feet on the different textures; he sits on a rock (p. 50), has the urge to jot down an impression and finds Mr. Deasy's letter with its blank end (p. 53), he looks at the boots Mulligan has given him (p. 54), he urinates (p. 55), picks his nose (p. 56) and turns to walk on to the city.

His desire to escape from history, personal and public, leads him to meditate on the nature of reality. The very first words of the chapter indicate that he is wondering how far his mind is tied to the world around him: 'Ineluctable modality of the visible' means roughly that you can't escape from that aspect of reality which is the visible world ('modality' can be taken to mean 'mode of existence'). He shuts his eyes as he walks along, half hoping that the world will not be there when he opens them. But he can't escape in that way. He is tied to space, the *nebeneinander* (German for 'next to one another'), as objects such as the rubbish washed up by the tide, even his own two feet, are. And the objects he sees are 'signatures' of time, relics of history, products in space of the *nacheinander* ('after one another'). Time and space hold him in an ineluctable, inescapable, grip. He is in fact walking blindfold into eternity (p. 43), and when he opens his eyes he sees two midwives carrying a bag which he imagines contains a still-born foetus with its navel-cord; in a dazzling flash of insight he sees this as part of an unending telephone cable connecting him to Adam, the first man, whose telephone number was Edenville 'Aleph, alpha, nought, nought one'. And Eve, of course, as the mediaeval theologians argued, had no navel, since she had no mother; her belly was without blemish.

So his thoughts proceed by associative leaps, and to pursue them in detail would naturally use more words than Joyce does. Here are a few cross-references to notice: his mother's ghost (p. 43) refers back to pp. 11, 16 and 34, 'an odour of wetted ashes'; his projected but unrealised visit to his uncle Richie Goulding (p. 44) is taken up by his father Simon on p. 90 in almost exactly the same phrases; the two midwives of p. 43 reappear on p. 50 and later on p. 143; Mulligan's song about Mary Ann 'hising up her petticoats' on p. 19 is remembered as Stephen sees the seaweed lifting on the tide (p. 55); the drowned man whose corpse is discussed on p. 27 surfaces in Stephen's mind on p. 55 (also 51); and most evocative of all, the three-masted schooner of the last sentence reappears on p. 249 and again on p. 545, where Stephen and Bloom meet a paid-off sailor from her, now drunk. It is with the moving image of this silent ship with its three crosstrees (? Calvary) that we say farewell to Stephen for the moment.

The Homeric parallel of Proteus is of use to remind us that this Egyptian sea-god assumed many shapes, modalities; so do Stephen's thoughts, so does the flowing sea which alters the surface of the shore, and so does language, one of time's most eloquent signatures. The 'art' of this chapter is Philology, and Stephen thinks in several languages—German, Latin, Italian, French, and even Romany (p. 53—'White thy fambles', etc.) Even the noise of his urination is a 'fourworded wave speech: seesoo, hrso, rsseeiss, ooos" (p. 55).

The solid earth on which he walks, 'These heavy sands are language tide and wind have silted here' (p. 50). Thus the sea, the land, history, language and existence are all ever changing yet almost incapable of being pinned down, as Menelaus found in his struggles with Proteus in the *Odyssey*.

Notice, too, in this chapter the many bits of Shakespeare, and particularly of *Hamlet*, which go to make up the coinage of Stephen's own language: to mention only four: nipping and eager airs (p. 44, l. 5), very like a whale (p. 46, l. 22), in sable silvered, Elsinore's tempting flood (p. 50, l. 13); and also the Hamlet hat (p. 53, l. 13).

And you will notice the *key* on p. 50, l. 7, and the *melon*, p. 52, l. 26, of which much more is to come.

Perhaps the most brilliant descriptive passage is that of the dog scampering and playing over the wide sands (pp. 51–2):

> a rag of wolf's tongue redpanting from his jaws. His speckled body ambled ahead of them and then loped off at a calf's gallop.

And perhaps the most important fact to emerge is that Stephen confirms himself in his decision to leave the tower and break with Mulligan, and become for the second time an exile:

> The cold domed room of the tower waits ... He has the key, I will not sleep there when this night comes ... Take all, keep all. My soul walks with me, form of forms.   p. 50

CHAPTER IV

Homeric parallel: Calypso.   Art: Home Economics.
Time: 8 a.m.   Place: Bloom's House.
Organ: Kidneys.   Symbol: Nymph.
Technique: Narrative (mature).

The only warning we get that there is a change of direction is the heading II on p. 57. The 'Telemachia' is finished and the story moves on to Odysseus himself. (It is not until p. 533, twelve chapters later, that Joyce prints the heading III.)

> Mr. Leopold Bloom ate with relish the inner organs of beasts and fowls.

Thus the new 'hero' is announced, an earthy man in contrast to the intellectual Stephen; and the long series of chapters related to the physical features of man begins. In this one Bloom goes out to buy his breakfast kidney, then fries it so carelessly that he burns it; then he eats it and goes to the lavatory. We soon realise that we are in a different mental climate, though we must not forget that Stephen too had a body (he urinated and he picked his nose in Chapter III, and we remember that he was troubled by lice in *A Portrait*). Bloom's mind has its obsessions, and we have to learn what they are, but its rhythm is more prosaic, its modes more factual. Stephen is a philosopher and poet, Bloom a scientist *manqué* and a practical man, though notably unsuccessful by worldly standards. Hence the Art celebrated in this chapter is Home Economics, or Domestic Economy. Bloom is shown as a domesticated husband who has got up to light the kitchen fire, takes his wife's breakfast to her in bed, feeds the cat, shops and cooks for himself; and his commercial mind takes pleasure in working out how much things cost, how other people make their money (on p. 60, for instance, he thinks about the prosperity of the publican O'Rourke, and on p. 68 he remembers his daughter's wages are 'twelve and six a week'— 62½p.).

Nevertheless he has his dreams. One of them is of an idyllic country life; as he walks after breakfast down the back garden to the privy, in his imagination the unkempt patch flourishes with runner beans, peas and lettuces, and Virginia creeper covers a summer-house (p. 70); the newspaper in which the butcher wraps the kidney displays an advertisement promoting the sale of shares in a planter's company in Palestine, which sets him off (p. 62) on a day-dream of 'quiet long days: pruning ripening', olive trees, lemons, oranges, melons. His day-dream of rural bliss comes up again as he undresses for bed on pp. 633–6.

But Bloom's chief preoccupation, we soon learn, is his wife Marion or Molly. It is '*her* breakfast' that he is preparing as early as line 7 on the first page, and her physical presence pervades the house and the bedroom as dominatingly as her image fills his mind for most of the chapter. The brass rings on the second-

Frank Budgen's drawing of Joyce and himself talking at a café table in Zürich. See p. 14.

The National Library, Dublin, as it was in Joyce's day. See *Ulysses*, Chapter IX.

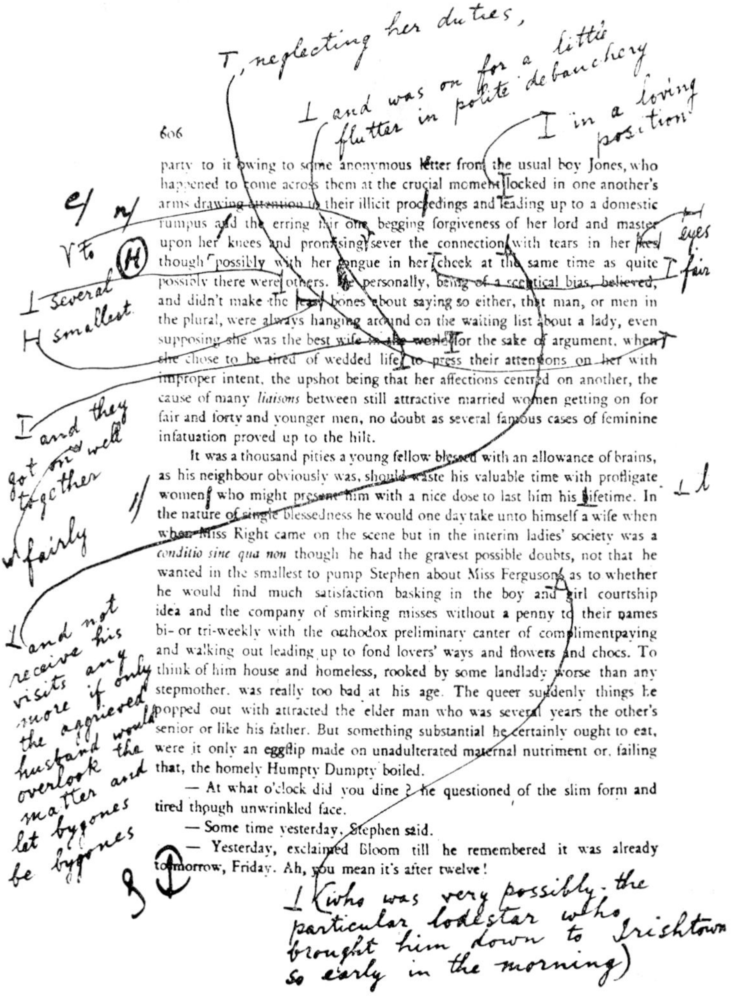

Handwritten annotations (top):

T, neglecting her duties,

↓ and was on for a little debauchery

flutter in polite

I in a loving position'

606

party to it owing to some anonymous letter from the usual boy Jones, who
happened to come across them at the crucial moment locked in one another's
arms drawing attention to their illicit proceedings and leading up to a domestic
rumpus and the erring fair one begging forgiveness of her lord and master
upon her knees and promising sever the connection with tears in her ~~eyes~~ eyes
though possibly with her tongue in her cheek at the same time as quite ~~fair~~
possibly there were others. He personally, ~~being of a sceptical bias, believed,~~
and didn't make the least bones about saying so either, that man, or men in
the plural, were always hanging around on the waiting list about a lady, even
supposing she was the best wife in the world ~~for the sake of argument, when~~
~~she chose to be tired of wedded life to press their attentions on her~~ with
improper intent, the upshot being that her affections centred on another, the
cause of many *liaisons* between still attractive married women getting on for
fair and forty and younger men, no doubt as several famous cases of feminine
infatuation proved up to the hilt.

It was a thousand pities a young fellow blessed with an allowance of brains,
as his neighbour obviously was, ~~should waste~~ his valuable time with profligate
women who might ~~present~~ him with a nice dose to last him his lifetime. In
the nature of ~~single~~ blessedness he would one day take unto himself a wife when
~~when~~ Miss Right came on the scene but in the interim ladies' society was a
conditio sine qua non though he had the gravest possible doubts, not that he
wanted in the smallest to pump Stephen about Miss Ferguson, as to whether
he would find much satisfaction basking in the boy and girl courtship
idea and the company of smirking misses without a penny to their names
bi- or tri-weekly with the orthodox preliminary canter of complimentpaying
and walking out leading up to fond lovers' ways and flowers and chocs. To
think of him house and homeless, rooked by some landlady worse than any
stepmother. was really too bad at his age. The queer suddenly things he
popped out with attracted the elder man who was several years the other's
senior or like his father. But something substantial he certainly ought to eat,
were it only an eggflip made on unadulterated maternal nutriment or, failing
that, the homely Humpty Dumpty boiled.

— At what o'clock did you dine ? he questioned of the slim form and
tired though unwrinkled face.

— Some time yesterday, Stephen said.

— Yesterday, exclaimed Bloom till he remembered it was already
tomorrow, Friday. Ah, you mean it's after twelve !

(Handwritten bottom): I (who was very possibly the
particular lodestar who
brought him down to Irishtown
so early in the morning)

Handwritten margin annotations (left): ℮ ny / V to / Ⓗ / I several / H smallest. / I and they / got on well / together / fairly / // / I and not / receive his / visits if only / more, any / the aggrieved / husband would / overlook the / matter and / let bygones / be bygones / 𝄞

Handwritten margin annotations (right): fair / fair / ↓ l / ↓ l

A page proof of part of *Ulysses* (Chapter XVI) corrected by Joyce.
See pp. 16 & 57.

James Joyce, B.A., 1902.

hand bedstead, bought by her father, Major Tweedy, in Gibraltar, jingle as she turns over in bed (p. 58) or sits up to drink her tea and eat the bread and butter that Bloom has prepared (p. 65). This jingling becomes one of the subjects of the fugue in the musical Chapter XI, 'The Sirens', where it is mingled with the jingle of the jaunty car in which Blazes Boylan rides to his assignation with Molly, in this very bed at four o'clock.

Over her bed hangs a cheap print of 'The Bath of the Nymph'. Odysseus was detained by the nymph Calypso, who like Molly Bloom had connections with Gibraltar; and Bloom is shown as a servant, a willing slave, of this modern nymph. Bloom mulls over her early life as daughter of a soldier stationed at Gibraltar (p. 58)—there is a lot more of this in Molly's final monologue (pp. 681, 700, 703, 704). He thinks of her 'ample bedwarmed flesh' as he walks along the street with his kidneys (p. 63). She is never far from his mind, and the reader soon suspects that he has odd sexual phantasies, and that these are connected with her underwear; he has in fact an underwear fetish; the first reference is to her new garters on p. 59, and many more are to come.

But other nymphs enter his consciousness. The next-door servant girl is before him in the pork-butcher's shop, and he frets at the butcher's slowness in serving him lest it should spoil his chance of following her along the street to enjoy the sight of her ample curves which have fascinated him as she whacked the mats on the line in the next-door garden (p. 61). His own daughter Milly sends him a letter by the morning post, and he thinks of her budding sexuality in a protective yet anxious way (pp. 68-9). Even the sunlight in the street is a nymph:

> Quick warm sunlight came running from Berkeley Road, swiftly, in slim sandals, along the brightening footpath. Runs, she runs to meet me, a girl with gold hair on the wind. p. 63

We also learn of Bloom's great sorrow at the death of his only son Rudy at the age of eleven days (p. 68); the gap left in his life cannot be filled, and the hunger it engenders is instrumental in making him yearn for Stephen (his Telemachus) when they finally meet in Chapter XIV (p. 388). Some sort of contact between the two is foreshadowed in the mention of Turko the Terrible on p. 59, who comes into Bloom's mind at about the same time as he enters Stephen's (p. 16); Chapters I and IV are contemporaneous, both beginning at eight o'clock.

Notice that Bloom forgets his *key* (p. 59); thinks about *cattle* (pp. 61, 70); and *seaside girls*, mentioned in Milly's letter (pp. 68–9), are a foreshadowing of Gerty MacDowell, the nymph of Chapter XIII.

Bloom's Jewishness is stressed, but not overstressed. One doesn't expect a man who fries himself a pork kidney in butter to be a Jew, but there are plenty of hints to be be picked up: the Wandering Jew who never grows older (p. 59, l. 18), who has obvious affinities with Odysseus and therefore with Bloom himself; the Jewish land settlement scheme; the cat's 'jewishness' in that it won't eat pork, only 'kosher' meat (p. 64).

Two remarkable pieces of writing are perhaps worth mentioning. The second is the incredibly daring—at the time—representation of Bloom's thoughts and sensations as he sits defecating on the cuckstool (pp. 71–2). But the first and even more remarkable is the sensitive depiction, largely by nuances and tones of voice, of Bloom's and Molly's relationship. This is shown best in the business of the letters that have come through the door while he was out.

> Two letters and a card lay on the hallfloor. He stopped and gathered them. Mrs. Marion Bloom. His quick heart slowed at once. Bold hand. Mrs. Marion . . .
> —Who are the letters for?
> He looked at them. Mullingar. Milly.
> —A letter for me from Milly, he said carefully, and a card to you. And a letter for you . . .
> Letting the blind up . . . his backward eye saw her glance at the letter and tuck it under her pillow . . .
> She was reading the card, propped on her elbow . . .
> He waited . . .
> But he delayed . . .

As he went down ... she called:
—Poldy!
—What?
—Scald the teapot.   pp. 63–4

A page later:

Nudging the door open with his knee he carried the tray in and
set it on the chair by the bedhead.
—What a time you were, she said.
She set the brasses jingling as she raised herself...
A strip of torn envelope peeped from under the dimpled pillow.
In the act of going he stayed to straighten the bedspread.
—Who was the letter from? he asked.
Bold hand. Marion.
—O, Boylan, she said...   p. 65

Notice how Bloom torments himself with the expectation of
Molly's adultery with Boylan, how he delays going downstairs,
how she makes time to read the letter by getting him to scald
the teapot and rinse it, how he *has* to ask who the letter was
from, how she puts indifference into her voice with '—O,
Boylan'. Whenever Boylan is mentioned in the rest of the book,
Bloom's heart misses a beat and he too strives to feign indifference or incomprehension. (We are reminded irresistibly of the
hero of *Exiles*, Richard Rowan.) And in the middle of this
cat-and-mouse game comes the cat herself (p. 64). This is
writing of great subtlety.

CHAPTER V

Homeric Parallel: Lotus-Eaters.   Arts: Botany and
Chemistry.   Time: 10 a.m.
Place: On the way to the Bath.   Organ: Genitals.
Symbol: Eucharist.   Technique: Narcissism.

The passage of time was marked by the clock of St. George's Church striking a quarter to nine at the end of the last chapter; Bloom's first appointment of the day is the funeral of Paddy Dignam at eleven, for which he has put on his black suit. Now it is ten o'clock and Bloom has an hour to spare for lotus-eating, *dolce far niente*, which he begins to enjoy on p. 73, where the Belfast and Oriental Tea Company's display window sets him thinking about the lazy East, where they 'sleep six months out of twelve'. Throughout this chapter Bloom's mind plays on narcotics, sweet smells, floating flowers. Though he carries out an occasional Bloomian calculation of profit (as with Lord Iveagh's porter-based fortune, p. 81) and thinks how he might have missed small advantages such as asking Tom Kernan to get him some tea (p. 73), or McCoy to wangle a railway pass to Mullingar where Milly is working, yet the atmosphere of the episode is lazy and self-indulgent. The warm morning (the thunder in the air of p. 69 is still present, slowly building up to its breaking in Chapter XIV, p. 392) induces lassitude and contentedness, and faithless Molly is not so insistently in his thoughts; she is supplanted by the silly Martha with whom Bloom is conducting a ridiculous clandestine correspondence, under the pseudonym of Henry Flower (which of course means Bloom). When he is finally able to get at the letter which was waiting for him at the Westland Row Post Office he finds a flower inside it. Botany is one of the Arts of this chapter, and allusions to flowers—blooms—take the most bizarre forms: Martha's headache is, he surmises, caused by 'her roses' (menstruation) (p. 80); the flowing beer which his lotus-eating imagination sees gushing from the huge barrels (p. 81) bears flowers of froth; and in the last paragraph he foresees his body lying in the bath, 'saw the dark tangled curls of his bush floating, floating hair of the stream around the limp father of thousands, a languid floating flower'.

The other art, Chemistry, is not the school subject with its factual scientific basis, but rather the art of the pharmacist and the perfumier. In Sweeny's chemist's shop he gets Molly's skin lotion made up and buys a tablet of lemon-scented soap. This he pockets, and it is encountered again at intervals during the day (pp. 102, 124, 183, 285, 373, 430, 432, 468 and 593). It performs a little *Odyssey* of its own right through the book.

Bloom does not actually get to the public bath-house in this chapter; he only thinks of it as a refuge where he can get rid of his sexual tensions, and cleanse his body. It is interesting that Stephen too (who we know hates water) thinks of the ministrations of female bath attendants (pp. 48–9) just as Bloom does (p. 86). Bloom has not had sexual intercourse with Molly since little Rudy died, so it is not surprising that he should seek relief in flirtation, however futile, and phantasy. One marvellously vivid passage in this chapter describes how he spies a well-to-do woman about to mount a high carriage, and his keen expectation of seeing an expanse of white stocking is balked by an intervening tramcar (pp. 75–6):

> Watch! Watch! Silk flash rich stockings white. Watch!
> A heavy tramcar honking its gong slewed between.
> Lost it. Curse your noisy pugnose. Feels locked out of it. Paradise and the peri. Always happening like that. The very moment.

Bloom encounters two acquaintances, one most significant for later chapters. The first is McCoy, a cadger carried over from the story 'Grace' in *Dubliners*. Bloom's sensitiveness about Molly's unfaithful heart is matched by his pride in her singing (which gives her the opportunity to be unfaithful, as with the impresario Boylan); when McCoy asks after Molly (p. 76) Bloom over-casually replies, but 'idly' unrolls the newspaper and reads 'idly' about an advertisement for Potted Meat (it is this delicacy that Boylan takes to the assignation with Molly, and whose flakes Bloom finds in her bed when he gets into it at the end of the day, p. 652). Bloom imagines her still in bed, 'not up yet', with the torn strip of envelope, and Boylan, who is 'getting it up', performing 'Love's Old Sweet Song' (a popular drawing-room ballad), an item in the repertoire for the projected tour (p. 65).

The second encounter is even more closely integrated into the 'story'. Bloom lets Bantam Lyons consult his paper on the form of the runners in the Ascot Gold Cup, to be run that afternoon, casually remarking he was going to 'throw it away' (p. 87). Now 'Throwaway' is the name of one of the horses, and Lyons, a typically superstitious punter, thinks Bloom is giving him a veiled tip, and rushes off to back it. He is dissuaded by another tipster, however; but when 'Throwaway' in fact wins, he spreads the canard that Bloom has had a spectacular win but is too mean to stand his friends a drink (pp. 178, 333 and 339). The word 'throwaway' meant an 'advertising handbill', and on p. 150 a sombre Y.M.C.A. young man hands one to Bloom, who throws it into the river, and we catch sight of it from time to time as it floats towards the sea.

The technique of the chapter is described as *Narcissism*, which is not so much a technique here as an ambiance. Narcissus was the beautiful youth who fell in love with his reflection in a pool; the drift of Bloom's thoughts is self-regarding in this chapter. For instance, he draws his hand 'with slow grace' (Bloom's self-conscious phrase as well as Joyce's) over his brow and hair as he inhales the fragrance of his hair-oil from his hat (p. 73); and nothing could be more narcissistic than the final sentence.

As for the symbol *Eucharist*, Bloom does actually enter a church (p. 82), witness a service of the Mass and meditate sceptically on the influence of the Church which is sustained by its rites. And Bloom finds his own lotus-eating peace in the ritual of the bath: 'This is my body,' he thinks.

CHAPTER VI

Homeric parallel: Hades.   Art: Religion.
Time: 11 a.m.   Place: Glasnevin Cemetery.
Organ: Heart.   Symbol: Caretaker.
Technique: Incubism.

The only heading of those above which presents any difficulty is the 'technique' of *Incubism*. This word could be derived from 'incubate', which can carry the meaning 'meditate, brood', or even 'lie down in a holy place in the hope of experiencing visions'; or from 'incubus', a nightmare or oppressive influence. Both words derive from the same Latin root, meaning 'to lie down upon'. Bloom certainly does a lot of brooding, on those who are lying in consecrated ground; and his mind is subject to the oppressive influence of death, as well as of the problems of his life. There is a constant direction of the thoughts downwards into the ground; even the bargeman standing on his barge in the lock as the funeral procession crosses the canal bridge is sinking downwards (p. 101); he is standing between the clamps of turf (peat) with which his barge is loaded, as if he were already in his grave, causing Bloom to brood on water-borne funerals, 'to heaven by water'.

By now Joyce's normal method is well established, if any of Joyce's methods can be called normal; this is the third chapter which is mostly conducted in Bloom's mind, as the first three were in Stephen's. There is a plunge straight into the funeral procession of Paddy Dignam, and the first page merits very careful reading and savouring; it is a fine piece of Joycean description and suggestion, and though it seems to state nothing, by the end of p. 89 we have picked up a lot of facts that a conventional writer would have set out in a studied description; at the same time we have imbibed the atmosphere of the carriage in which Bloom and three friends, or rather acquaintances, are riding; and of course Bloom's mind has been explored in greater detail.

The first part of the chapter, as far as p. 102, takes place in a carriage of the cortège; four men's personalities are shown interacting as they pass along the Dublin street, see people they know outside, and make appropriate conversation. It is soon apparent that Bloom has no really close friends. In this chapter come several Dubliners (some of whom have already figured in the short stories) and none of them seems to accept Bloom fully: he is an alien, almost an outcast.

Simon Dedalus, Stephen's egregious father, is one of the four;

he has gone even further downhill into seediness since *A Portrait*: he is a wit and a raconteur, with a vigorous turn of phrase, but he breaks down in maudlin self-pity over his wife's recent grave—not an edifying sight (p. 106). He appears again and again in the book, and always in unflattering circumstances. Stephen too is glimpsed as the carriage passes him (p. 89). It is Bloom who spots him, and we may note the beginning of the connection in Bloom's mind between Stephen and his own lost son Rudy (p. 90). This is to be one of the main themes of the book, the human relationship between father and son, and Bloom's vain attempt to put Stephen in little Rudy's place.

Not only is Rudy present in Bloom's brooding mind (see also pp. 97 and 113), but also his dead father, who had committed suicide (p. 98) in the hotel he kept in Ennis (p. 103). And as the carriage proceeds through the city, other sights stimulate thoughts of death, burial and the underworld: the rippedup roadway on p. 89, the dogs' home (reminder of Bloom's father's dog, and an oblique reference to Odysseus' dog, and to Cerberus the dog who guards the gates of Hades (p. 92)), another funeral (p. 97), Our Lady's Hospice for the dying (p. 99), cattle about to be slaughtered (p. 99), a house where a murder has been committed (p. 101).

But Bloom's living problem obtrudes, too. Just as he is thinking of Boylan ('He's coming in the afternoon. Her songs') the other three salute him as he stands on the sidewalk with hat raised in respect for the corpse; and the dandy Boylan flashes the white disc of his dressy straw hat in reply. Bloom makes no sign, but studies his nails, until he can face his companions with a 'vacant glance', expecting their probing questions, that might or might not be innocent (Power's interest might, he concludes, be 'only politeness perhaps', p. 95, l. 19).

Bloom's foreignness, his self-effacing manner and lack of status are all displayed in the incident of the Jewish moneylender, Reuben J. Dodd, neatly and succinctly described:

> A tall blackbearded figure, bent on a stick, stumping round the corner of Elvery's elephant house showed them a curved hand open on his spine.   p. 95

The three curse or mock him, but Bloom, self-consciously of the same race, tries to jump in with a good story about Reuben, only to be interrupted and have his joke ruined by Martin Cunningham. Bloom is again rejected on the last page of the chapter, in connection with John Henry Menton's hat (*hat*, you will remember, is one of the repeated symbols of the book, like the *keys* on pp. 108 and 109, and the organic symbol *heart* on pp. 97, 107, 115).

The diligent student of Homer can, of course, find many allusions to Odysseus' descent into Hades, but the chapter speaks its grisly message plainly enough without the help of the *Odyssey*. But one or two other neat connections with the rest of the book are worth noting: the navel-cord of p. 43 reappears on p. 114; the swirling maggots (p. 110) remind Bloom of Boylan's 'seaside girls' song (p. 68); the bee-sting that Bloom got on Whit Monday in his back garden (p. 70) was attended to in the hospital for the dying by a student (p. 99) who later invites Bloom into the common room of the lying-in hospital (p. 384); a plum-seller by Nelson's pillar (p. 96) sells her fruit in Stephen's anecdote on p. 146; and most of the many people seen on the streets or mentioned in the conversation play their parts in later episodes: for example, Richie Goulding, Ben Dollard and Hynes the reporter.

Two odd features of the chapter are the man in the brown mackintosh who makes the thirteenth at the graveside, whom Bloom inadvertently christens in the newspaper report (p. 113) and who makes several appearances in his mind during the day; and the use by Joyce of Martha's spelling mistake in her letter to 'Henry Flower': 'I do not like that other world [meaning *word*]' (p. 79). Bloom's last morbid, even perverted, thoughts, as he emerges through the gates of the cemetery end thus:

> There is another world after death named hell. I do not like that other world she wrote. No more do I. Plenty to see and hear and feel yet. Feel live warm beings near you.

Thus after all the characteristic calculations of numbers of dead, methods of ensuring that people are not buried alive,

81

gramophone records of great-grandfather, swirling maggots and well-fed graveyard rats, Bloom's mind throws off the incubus, and he returns, his usual kindly but rejected self, to the world of hats and bed-warmed flesh.

CHAPTER VII

Homeric parallel: Aeolus.   Art: Rhetoric.
Time: 12 noon.   Place: The *Freeman* Newspaper Office.
Organ: The Lungs.   Symbol: Editor.
Technique: Enthymemic.

Now Joyce begins to vary his method and his style in a way that readers ignorant of the book's scheme find completely bewildering. Having got used to the mixture of narrative and interior monologue, developed in three chapters seen through Stephen's eyes and three through Bloom's, we suddenly come upon a couple of pages which are split up by what appear to be newspaper headlines (pp. 118–19); then follow collections of words and names rather than sentences, and they are not the words of Bloom or of Stephen, but of some windy rhetorician writing for effect: the trams 'slowed, shunted, changed trolley, started'; 'right and left parallel clanging ringing a double-decker and a single-deck moved from their railheads, swerved to the down line, glided parallel'. The red tramcars are shown to be circulating to the extremities of 'The Hibernian Metropolis' from its 'heart', at Nelson's pillar. So the heart's blood circulates through the lungs, carrying new life to the extremities of the body. In the next paragraph, under the similarly inflated heading 'The Wearer of the Crown', His Majesty's vermilion mail cars are being loaded not just with 'mail', but 'letters, postcards, lettercards, parcels, insured and paid, for local, provincial, British and overseas delivery'.

This is ridiculously exaggerated writing, in keeping with

journalistic pomposity, using too many words and straining for effect. That is the joke. In this chapter dozens of rhetorical devices are used, and diligent scholars have particularised them, just as they have with Shakespeare's. In Joyce's days schoolboys and girls had to learn to recognise them; in ancient Rome schools of rhetoric taught the patricians how to make effective speeches by employing them; students of Chaucer's *Franklin's Tale* will have come across them as 'figures'; but in our degenerate days we can recognise only half a dozen because we are obsessed with the sloppy generic term 'image'. Joyce crammed into this chapter as many figures as he could manage, and it may be amusing to spot some of them.

Through the chapter a breeziness persists. Aeolus was the king of the winds and blew Odysseus in unplanned directions. So Bloom meets with the caprice of the editor of the *Freeman* newspaper; first he is encouraged in his quest of an advertisement for the paper (p. 131), and then rudely brushed off when he returns to ask help from the editor (pp. 138 and 147): 'Tell him he can kiss my arse.' Windy words, and references to windy actions, are numerous; on p. 127 at least seven expressions refer to wind or breath; in the newspaper office doors are flung violently open, tissues rustle, men puff smoke, newsboys rush down stairs into the street yelling, their papers fluttering. All the rush, bustle and vitality of a newspaper office is vividly portrayed: it is truly the lungs of the city, breathing in and blowing out ideas and information with a tremendous air of self-importance. Yet it is an inflated importance, self-created and self-regarding.

The characters who are gathered in the office, waiting on the editor, discuss the art of rhetoric: Ned Lambert mocks the slushy prose of the newspaper's country correspondent (pp. 125–7); J. J. O'Molloy, a briefless barrister, admires a highly-mannered sentence spoken by a famous K.C. about Michelangelo's Moses (p. 141); MacHugh, a seedy scholar dubbed 'professor', quotes at great length a speech about Moses delivered at a historical society meeting (p. 142–4); finally Stephen in effect puts them in their place by his *Dubliners*-type story about the two old women who climbed the Nelson monument and spat their plum-stones between the railings: this enigmatically unexciting tale may be taken as a deliberate contrast to the high-flown prose admired by the pundits—a lesson, if you like, in the new style of matter-of-fact portrayal of ordinary people's lives and preoccupations, modern naturalism or social realism.

It does not help much to know that the chapter's technique is *enthymemic*. An enthymeme is an argument based on improbable premisses, or a syllogism with one premiss missing. Perhaps Joyce is drawing attention to the atmosphere of inconclusive debate that permeates the chapter.

The newspaper headlines can be seen to progress from dignified Victorian ones: IN THE HEART OF THE HIBERNIAN METROPOLIS, to ridiculous American-style jokey ones: DIMINISHED DIGITS PROVE TOO TITILLATING FOR FRISKY FRUMPS. No doubt this gave Joyce much amusement, but the joke may seem rather laboured to modern readers.

It is a help to the reader to see the chapter in three separate sections. From p. 118 to p. 128 (l. 6) the action takes place in the mind of Bloom. At that point ordinary Joycean narrative begins, extending to p. 133, when Stephen enters the office. From p. 133 to p. 150 the mind of Stephen takes over.

In part 1, pp. 118–28, Bloom is earning his living; he is trying to arrange a three-month run of the Alexander Keyes advertisement, which entails getting the editor to insert a 'puff' (another windy word which means a favourable editorial reference) into the news columns (p. 122), and designing a little emblem of crossed keys as a sort of trade-mark of the firm of Keyes. Bloom has to speak to Red Murray, presumably in charge of the outer office where Bloom gets a copy of the current Keyes advertisement, to Nannetti, the printing foreman and a City Councillor; then to the editor himself (p. 130). Bloom's mind is engaged with these business activities along with his other preoccupations: his Jewishness emerges for a moment when he sees a typesetter distributing the letters which he has to read backwards, as Bloom's father read his Hebrew devotional books (p.

124); on the same page he re-stows the lemon soap and thinks of Martha and Molly; on p. 121 he tries unsuccessfully to remind Hynes, the reporter, of a three-week-old debt of three shillings; the essential niceness of his nature, his consideration for other people's feelings born of his own uncertain status among his acquaintances, is shown on p. 122 when he contemplates asking the Italian-named Nannetti how to pronounce the word *voglio* (pp. 65 and 66) which comes in Molly's duet *La ci darem* from *Don Giovanni*: in itself a significant song for Molly, who is about to yield to Blazes Boylan as Zerlina in the opera does to Don Juan (*voglio* means 'I will'); but Bloom decides not to in case Nannetti would be hurt if in spite of his Italian name he couldn't speak Italian. Bloom's alienness is glanced at by the professor on p. 126:

> —Most pertinent question, the professor said between his chews.
> With an accent on the whose.

And Bloom is mocked by the newsboys outside, and by the professor and Lenehan inside the office as he walks away:

> Both smiled over the crossblind at the file of capering newsboys in Mr. Bloom's wake, the last zigzagging white on the breeze a mocking kite, a tail of white bowknots. p. 131

Part 3 of this chapter is Stephen's. He has come to the newspaper to deliver Mr. Deasy's letter about foot-and-mouth disease (pp. 37–9), which was truncated when he needed a piece of paper to jot down his inspiration (p. 53). He is welcomed as an aspirant to literature and asked by the editor to write for him. Here is a neat flash-back to *A Portrait*; Myles Crawford says,

> You can do it. I can see it in your face. *In the lexicon of youth* . . .
> See it in your face. See it in your eye. Lazy idle little schemer.

So Stephen recalls the words of the harsh prefect of studies when he canes him for having broken his glasses (p. 50 of *A Portrait*).

Stephen's mind plays on *Hamlet* (pp. 140 and 142) (which prepares us again for his disquisition on Shakespeare in Chapter IX) as well as on his mother's death and on the art of verse.

Many things which he thought about in Chapters I–III recur here, and it is in this chapter, shared with Bloom, that the two nearly meet. Stephen, a chip of the old block, the son of a spendthrift father, invites all the older men to help him drink his hard-earned wages from Mr. Deasy (p. 144), and Bloom, coming back to get the editor's consent to the 'little puff' which will clinch for him the Keyes advertising deal, sees Stephen leading the older—and nearly penniless—men to the pub. Bloom's heart goes out in pity for the careless but attractive youth (p. 147). This is a foretaste of their relationship that will eventually end the book.

This chapter has many brilliant passages. I like particularly the flavour, so unerringly captured, of literary—or rather journalistic—talk, especially in the middle section of narrative (pp. 128–33). Another vivid portrait is that of the sponger Lenehan (whom we first met in that very nasty story 'Two Gallants' in *Dubliners*) at work cadging cigarettes by being ready with his matches (pp. 132 and 141), and making asinine facetious word-jokes, such as 'Thanky-vous', 'Able was I ere I saw Elba', the ghastly pun about 'Rose of Castille', and 'Clamn dever'. One sentence among dozens of vivid ones is unforgettable in its descriptive power: 'Witless shellfish swam in the gross lenses to and fro, seeking outlet.' Who but Joyce could so catch the exact words, the exact metaphor, for a short-sighted man's thinking eyes behind their glasses?

It may help the reader to note here one or two more cross-references. First of all, the paper's official tip for the Gold Cup—Sceptre; see pp. 173–4, and of course 87 for Throwaway. Next the story of Skin-the-Goat and the Phoenix Park murder, p. 137, which links up with pp. 533 and 542. Then a couple of minor ones: on p. 143 the cigarette smoke reminds Stephen of a line from *Cymbeline* which comes into his mind again at the end of Chapter IX (p. 218); and there is another reference on p. 143—'By the Nilebank the babemaries kneel, cradle of bulrushes'—to Moses in the bulrushes, who occurred to Stephen in Chapter III (p. 50). So the book is continually unified, and so the thought-paths of an active mind are portrayed in revealing detail.

CHAPTER VIII

Homeric parallel: The Lestrygonians.
Art: Architecture.   Time: 1 p.m. (lunchtime).
Place: The Restaurants.   Organ: Digestive Tract.
Symbol: Constables.   Technique: Peristaltic.

After the windy bustle of the newspaper office, this chapter
returns to Bloom's own mind as he walks through the streets
thinking of his lunch; the term 'peristaltic' refers to the wave-
like spasmodic motion of the food through the digestive tract,
and this is how Bloom moves through the streets, accepting a
religious handbill, a *throwaway* (p. 150), feeding the seagulls (p.
152), meeting an old flame (p. 156), seeing the barmy Farrell
looping his walk round the lamp-posts (p. 159), passing a squad
of constables (p. 162), hearing a snatch of the conversation of the
poet A.E. (George Russell, already mentioned on p. 141 in
connection with Stephen, who, as Joyce himself did at Stephen's
age, had visited him to talk mysticism and literature in the small
hours), stopping to test whether his little finger, held at arm's
length, covers the sun's disk (p. 166), entering the Burton
restaurant and being sickened by the sight of men chewing (p.
168), eating a vegetarian lunch at Davy Byrne's, walking on to
the National Library and helping a blind youth (whom we meet
later as a piano-tuner in the 'Sirens' chapter) across the street,
and finally retreating into the Museum to avoid his enemy
Boylan. It will be seen that this halting, uncontrolled physical
movement, taken together with the play of his thoughts and the
demands of his stomach, are perhaps comparable to the process
of digestion—itself detailed on p. 176:

> And we stuffing food in one hole and out behind: food, chyle,
> blood, dung, earth, food: have to feed it like stoking an engine.

Just as the metaphors of the 'Aeolus' chapter refer to winds, so
in this peristaltic chapter Joyce draws on the vocabulary of food
and eating. On any one page there are half a dozen phrases. The

sights that impinge on Bloom's mind are also connected with eating and defecating: he sees a dog being sick and returning to his vomit (p. 179), the blind youth has food-stains on his coat (p. 181), he passes a plumber's window full of lavatory pans, 'waiting' (p. 179); and the chapter begins with a 'sugarsticky girl shovelling scoopfuls of creams' in a sweet shop called Lemon's (p. 150).

Apart from this preoccupation with food, the chapter is much like the earlier Bloom chapters, IV–VI. It takes place almost entirely in the mind of Bloom, the only exception being pp. 176–9, when Joyce again provides a dazzling picture of bar-room conversation among half a dozen cronies, as brilliant as the conversation in the newspaper office. The preoccupations of Bloom's mind are fascinating. Several times he shows kindly consideration for others: he pities the rags of Stephen's mother-less sister (p. 151), buys Banbury cakes to feed the ravenous seagulls (p. 152), looks sympathetically on poor Mrs. Breen (p. 157), meditates with compassion on the labour of women (p. 161), helps the blind youth while striving not to talk down to him for his being unable to see.

> Say something to him. Better not do the condescending. They mistrust what you tell them. Pass a common remark . . .

Bloom's marital problem too recurs during the chapter. Sometimes memories of happier days light up his brooding, but on three major occasions, among several minor ones, the hated Boylan causes his mind to shudder. The first is on p. 153, when he thinks of venereal disease and hopes horrifyingly that Boylan is not infected; the second is when Nosey Flynn lives up to his name by asking about Molly and her forthcoming concert tour with Boylan—Bloom's deliberate pauses and hesitations on p. 172 are eloquent, as we saw in Chapter VI (p. 94); and lastly Bloom spots the swell Boylan—

> Straw hat in sunlight. Tan shoes. Turnedup trousers. It is. It is. His heart quopped softly . . .

—and escapes an encounter by turning into the Museum (p. 183).

Bloom's underwear fetish also obtrudes in this chapter. Among several references the most famous one is that on which Joyce spent a whole day—page 168. But he also notices the loose stockings on the frumpish girl talking to A.E. (p. 165), who later recurs on p. 370. And when he has idly calculated the commission on the Keyes advertisement, he thinks generously he can buy Molly a silk petticoat to match her garters, only to be stabbed to the heart with the realisation that Boylan will be the one to see them next—'Today. Today. Not think' (p. 180).

Bloom's lack of education is also displayed. He thinks of parallax, the understanding of which is essential to a study of the movements of the stars in astronomy (p. 153), and which recurs in the pseudo-scientific Chapter XVII (p. 619), but he doesn't fully understand it, any more than Molly does metempsychosis. He puzzles about the Italian of *Don Giovanni*, not knowing what *teco* (with you) means (p. 179).

The throwaway pamphlet of the first page (p. 150) is tossed into the Liffey just before he feeds the seagulls, and is to reappear on its voyage to the sea (pp. 226, 239, 249, etc.); but it is also a reminder of the horse Throwaway that later wins the Gold Cup, and is obliquely referred to by Bantam Lyons (who thought Bloom had given him this tip on p. 87) on p. 179.

But the *pièce de résistance* is the sickening description of the gross-feeding men in the Burton restaurant. The Homeric parallel of this chapter is the Lestrygonian tribe of cannibals, whose eating habits shock all right-thinking people. Bloom is not a vegetarian or a teetotaller (he despises both fads, pp. 165 and 161), and we know he likes a fried kidney; but today the impact of seeing 'the animals feed' is too much for him, and Joyce writes it so that it is almost too much for the reader:

> Spaton sawdust, sweetish warmish cigarette smoke, reek of plug [tobacco], spilt beer, men's beery piss, the stale of ferment.
>
> p. 169

No wonder his gorge rose.

We cannot but admire, however, the immense skill needed to bring off such a repulsive triumph. It is, of course, necessary for readers to feel what Bloom feels—not enough merely to see what he sees and think what he thinks. Consider the eight words which describe the application of mustard to a strip of cheese sandwich: 'He studded under each lifted strip yellow blobs' (p. 172). This is not only a miracle of economy and a clear image; it is part of Bloom's deliberate concentration on a physical neutral act while his feelings are agitated by Nosey Flynn's prying after Molly's relationship with Boylan, and his mind is devising the nonchalant answer that will not give him away.

CHAPTER IX

Homeric parallel: Scylla and Charybdis.
Art: Literature.   Time: 2 p.m.
Place: The National Library.   Organ: The Brain.
Symbols: Stratford, London.
Technique: Dialectic (Socratic).

Stephen conducts, in this least interesting chapter of the whole book, a long dialectical argument on the supreme play of the supreme figure of our literature; his listeners, or opponents, or butts, are (for the first nine pages) A.E. (George Russell) the poet, and three of the top members of the Library's staff: Lyster the director, Best, his eventual successor, who had translated a French book on the Irish legends, and Magee, who under the pseudonym of John Eglinton edited the intellectual journal *Dana*, named after an Irish earth-goddess. These four literary men, *real people*, represent for Joyce (as for Stephen) the Celtic twilight, one facet of the provincial nationalism of Dublin which he hated and despised (see p. 11). Stephen has already demonstrated his superiority to the journalists; now he puts a somewhat fanciful case, though based on a good deal of know-ledge, about Shakespeare's relationship with Hamlet—he 'proves by algebra that Hamlet's grandson is Shakespeare's grandfather', as Mulligan has said on p. 24; and Buck Mulligan joins in the discussion in his mocking ribald way when he enters the Librarian's room on p. 197 with the facetious yet sarcastic 'Amen!' as Stephen is in full flow on the central theme of the son's consubstantiality with the father.

This meeting of minds is just as vividly realised as the other conversation pieces already noticed: Bloom in the funeral carriage, the journalists in the newspaper office, and the friends in Davy Byrne's. But this time the Brain is the organ, Literature the art celebrated, and the method Socratic. The characters stand out as individuals; Lyster is a Quaker and his boots creak as he walks deferentially in and out on library business; Eglinton pretends to common sense and pits the no-nonsense point of view against Stephen's more imaginative leaps in argument; and Best is tentative and urbane; while A.E. spouts his particular brand of mysticism that Stephen detests but is reluctant to pillory, since he is conscious of owing Russell money: 'A.E.I.O.U.', as he wittily thinks on p. 190.

Stephen's case is mainly that Shakespeare saw himself as Hamlet's father rather than, as was generally supposed in those days of romantic criticism, Hamlet the young prince. With a dazzling display of factual—and conjectural—knowledge of the details of Shakespeare's life, and a vast number of quotations and references from the plays and from literature in general, as well as from the Church Fathers, Stephen builds a shaky but impressive edifice which yet fails to convince his hearers. Nor is he himself convinced of his own conclusions; like Joyce, he takes pleasure in the doing, yet finishes up just as unsettled in his opinions as in his whole mode of life. On the subject of paternity he says:

A father is a necessary evil ... Fatherhood, in the sense of conscious begetting, is unknown to man ... Paternity may be a legal fiction. Who is the father of any son that any son should love him or he any son?' p. 207

Certainly Stephen has little reason to love his own father Simon. Besides this theme of paternity, central to this book as to the

Odyssey and to Christian Theology, Stephen also talks of cuck-oldry, producing the remarkably plausible theory that Ann Hathaway, Shakespeare's seductive wife, bedded with one of his brothers, Edmund or Richard, while he was away in London; and adduces as evidence the fact that Edmund and Richard are names of Shakespeare's arch-villains. Cuckoldry is, of course, a preoccupation of Bloom's, and another of the book's central themes, as it is of *Exiles*.

As in most of the chapters of the book, the theme of Jewishness recurs; and right in the middle (p. 200) the Jew-Greek Bloom enters the Library to search the files of the *Kilkenny People* newspaper for an advertisement: 'a patient silhouette . . . a bow-ing dark figure'. Mulligan has seen him examining the marble statues of goddesses in the Museum to discover if they have mortal anuses (as he pondered on p. 176, lines 26–7), and describes him as 'Greeker than the Greeks'. When Mulligan and Stephen leave (p. 217) Bloom passes between them, 'bowing, greeting', as they hesitate over their next movements. For the second time Bloom nearly accosts Stephen, and this time what he is thinking is evident both from a previous glance into his mind (p. 147) and from Mulligan's words:

> The wandering Jew . . . Did you see his eye?
> He looked upon you to lust after you. I fear thee, ancient mariner.
> O, Kinch, thou art in peril. p. 217

At the same moment Stephen is remembering how he watched the birds for augury from this very portico (*P.A.Y.M.* pp. 224–6). This is only one of several references back to *A Portrait* that serve to link the two books.

But to the average reader—to anyone except a student of the history of Shakespearean criticism—this long chapter, stuffed with literary references, is bound to be tedious. Modern or at any rate Leavisite criticism would in general side with the des-pised A.E. when he objects (p. 189) that

> This prying into the family life of a great man . . . [is] . . . inter-esting only to the parish clerk . . . We have *King Lear*: and it is immortal.

Of course we finish the chapter with a deeper knowledge of Stephen's subtle and tenacious intellect, and incidentally of his preoccupations with such things as his mother's death and his inability to feel at home in the prevailing Dublin literary scene; but the price is exorbitant; only a Shakespearean scholar can pick up the myriad references to the plays, to the facts of and gossip about Shakespeare's life. True, Joyce varies the texture by short passages in other modes than the dialectic prose and stream of Stephen's consciousness: there is a dramatic section on p. 209, a page of free verse on p. 203, Mulligan's bawdy rhymes, and the Dramatis Personae of his rude play (pp. 216–7).

One important generalisation stands out for its relevance to Joyce's own life:

> —The world believes that Shakespeare made a mistake, [Eglinton] said, and got out of it as quickly and as best he could [in leaving Ann Hathaway for London].
> —Bosh! Stephen said rudely. A man of genius makes no mistakes. His errors are volitional and are the portals of discovery.   p. 190

It would appear that Joyce's own life was one long attempt to recover from error after error committed in blind ignorance of the everyday necessities of life. Yet from his 'mistakes' comes the great work that is the subject of this study fifty years later. Clearly his errors too were the portals of discovery.

The narrative of the events of Stephen's day is carried on, obliquely as ever, in the chapter. On p. 29 Haines, the Oxford folklore-hunter, and Mulligan make a date with Stephen for twelve-thirty in the Ship Inn. At that time Stephen was buying drinks for the newspapermen in quite another place, and by 2 p.m. he is in the Library. He has sent Mulligan a telegram (p. 185) quoting from George Meredith, at that date the fashionable novelist in intellectual circles. When Mulligan catches Stephen in the Library (p. 199) he reads out the telegram, then whines in a parody of Synge's Irish dramatic language his complaint at being stood up. Haines, too, has been in the Library but has gone off in search of a book of folklorish poems (p. 186), having been shown this and the French book by Jubainville that Best had (in real life) translated. When the two young men leave the Library, we again see that Stephen is trying to bring the friendship to an end:

Part. The moment is now.   p. 217

Finally, it remains to say that the relevance of Scylla and Charybdis to this chapter is a matter of much dispute. Odysseus sailed, not without loss, between these two hazards, but what the hazards are that Stephen (or Bloom) negotiates are by no means clear. Perhaps Stephen steers between the rock of dogma (or fact) and the whirlpool of mysticism (or imaginative interpretation) in both theology and the study of Shakespeare. But one can only conclude that little illumination is afforded by this Homeric parallel.

CHAPTER X

Homeric parallel: The Wandering Rocks.
Art: Mechanics.   Time: 3 p.m.
Place: The Streets of Dublin.   Organ: The Blood.
Symbol: Citizens.   Technique: Labyrinthine.

After two 'normal' chapters Joyce now launches into a most puzzling labyrinth in which nineteen short sections, varying from half a page to half a dozen in length, are juxtaposed with varying degrees of interconnection. The Wandering Rocks are not one of Odysseus' hazards (as was said on p. 58) but they certainly are to the reader of *Ulysses*. There is no clue on p. 218 that we are beginning anything other than an ordinary chapter of thirty or forty pages; we read of Father Conmee (an old friend from *A Portrait*) who has been asked by Martin Cunningham (see the 'Hades' chapter, VI) to find a school place for Master Patrick Aloysius Dignam, whose father has just been buried. We share the Rector of Clongowe's thoughts and dreams, and meet the people he meets and see the sights of the Dublin streets, for six pages. Then suddenly there is a switch to Corny Kelleher and his daybook; but even in this half-page intrudes unaccountably a generous white arm (Molly's) in a window in Eccles Street, just as in the middle of Father Conmee's thoughts Mr. Dennis J. Maginni, professor of dancing, has walked dressed to the nines (p. 219), and Corny Kelleher's funeral establishment has been passed (p. 220). It is indeed a labyrinth that is being presented—and a labyrinth in which many citizens of Dublin and the two main characters of the book walk about aimlessly or purposefully.

It is useful to number the nineteen sections in your copy of the book, and in this short analysis I will refer to these numbers rather than to pages.

First let us look briefly at the progress of the 'story'. Bloom appears in episode 10. He is looking for a book for Molly, whose tastes apparently run to the erotic; he samples *Sweets of Sin*, whose luscious prose starts up sexual phantasy in his mind, which recurs later in the book—'For him! For Raoul!' (p. 262) and 'felt for the curves inside her *déshabillé*' (p. 366). He has already read books by the original masochist (Leopold von Sacher-Masoch) and another called *Fair Tyrants* by John Lovebirch; and in the surrealist fantasy of Chapter XV Bloom's masochism is confirmed—though by now we are fairly cognisant of it. Bloom is also referred to in episode 15, where it is shown that he has subscribed freely to the fund Martin Cunningham is getting up for the Dignams; and in episode 9, where Lenehan (just after mentioning that Bantam Lyons had a hot tip for the Gold Cup, Bloom's Throwaway, but had persuaded him to back Sceptre) sees Bloom looking at books on a hawker's cart, not knowing it is he who had 'tipped' Throwaway. Another Bloom, a dentist, is mentioned in episode 17, but this is just a confusing blind turn such as you find in any labyrinth.

Boylan occupies episode 5, where he is choosing fruit to send to Molly with a bottle wrapped in pink tissue paper and a jar of

Plumtree's Potted Meat (with which home is an abode of bliss) (pp. 76 and 604), for the seduction feast after four o'clock. The sketch of Boylan the lady-killer is beautifully done, as he takes a red carnation and puts it between his teeth while he ogles the girl shop assistant and peers at her plump breasts. The typist in Boylan's office (episode 7) is also heard making his afternoon free of appointments from four (after he has met Lenehan in the Ormond bar and restaurant) till after six.

Molly's generous white arm (she is in *déshabillé*) flings money from the window of No. 7 Eccles Street (episode 2) to the one-legged sailor who received only a blessing from Father Conmee in episode 1. Her arm is seen again putting back in the window whence she had dislodged it a card announcing *Unfurnished Apartments*. The Blooms are looking for a sub-tenant or lodger, and Stephen is later offered accommodation but declines it (p. 616). Molly's gaminess is discussed in episode 9 but she does not appear in the book till her own, final, chapter.

Stephen is shown in episode 6 talking to his music teacher about discontinuing singing lessons (Joyce had a fine voice and like John McCormack could have made his way as a tenor soloist). In episode 13 he meets his sister Dilly (who is still part of the disintegrating motherless family, shown in episode 4) at a bookstall; his father Simon has already met Dilly outside the auction rooms where they were selling the family curtains, worth two guineas, for five shillings (25p.). (The handbell of the lacquey by the door of Dillon's auction rooms mingles its note with the last lap bell of the cyclists contesting the half-mile sprint outside the College Library: another twist of the labyrinth—or another rock that wanders into the path of the navigating reader.)

Stephen is mentioned also in episode 16, where Buck Mulligan and Haines takes tea with scones, butter and cakes at the D.B.C. (Dublin Bread Company, but 'damn bad cakes' according to the mocker Mulligan). It is Stephen who most of all explores and expounds the 'Mechanics', the Art of the chapter. He stands by the powerhouse in episode 13 and hears the whirr, hum and throb of the machinery, which echoes in his mind as the swirling worlds of the universe, or the whirlpools of his unsettled, questing soul. Joyce is reputed to have written this chapter with a street-map of Dublin before him and a stop-watch in his hand; so intricate is the labyrinth, so dependent on the mechanism of a perfect machine. And apart from the many references in each episode to other episodes, that come upon the reader like rocks that wander into his course, the *throwaway* of the Y.M.C.A. young man of p. 150 continues its journey to the sea, a band of Highland soldiers assembles in preparation for playing 'My girl's a Yorkshire girl,' a pop favourite of the day; the viceregal cavalcade is glimpsed in several episodes before it eventually traverses the city, passing most of the characters in the chapter, in the final episode.

So this mechanistic, labyrinthine, obstacle-studded chapter of nineteen sections comes to an end. I have been able only to indicate a few of the cross-references. In its totality, however, the chaotic chapter epitomises the teeming, vital, interlocked quality of life in general. It is significant that in the final episode, where the viceroy, Lord Dudley, progresses through the lively Dublin streets, saluting and being saluted by most of the citizens, from the two midwives of p. 43 to Almidano Artifoni of p. 227, Bloom himself does not appear, nor does Stephen. If you or I had been writing this chapter, that sums up in its form and content the whole book, we would have had Bloom salute the viceroy, so rounding off the presentation of a complete city. But not Joyce; to him life is not a tidy artefact, though it might be said that *Finnegans Wake* is an attempt to make it one.

CHAPTER XI

Homeric parallel: Sirens.   Art: Music.   Time: 4 p.m.
Place: The Ormond Hotel Concert Room.
Organ: The Ear.   Symbol: Barmaids.
Technique: *Fuga per Canonem.*

At first sight this is the most bewildering chapter so far. It begins with nearly two pages of unrelated and unintelligible snippets. The reader might, if he is very alert, recognise the first three words: 'Bronze by gold'. At the top of p. 252, and before that on p. 245, Miss Kennedy and Miss Douce, the barmaids in the Ormond Hotel, raise their heads, one bronze and one gold, above the cross-blind of their bar window to see the viceregal cavalcade pass by. Now they are *hearing* the steelyringing hoof-irons, for this is a musical chapter, and most of the fifty-odd snippets on the first two pages imitate the sounds—notes or themes or motifs—of the complicated canonic fugue that starts on p. 256, l. 8, with the word 'Begin!'. Some of the motifs (the most convenient word, though not an exact equivalent of the musical term) are easily recognised, because they refer to incidents or thoughts that are already familiar, like the first seven words. But most of them refer to sounds whose relevance is still to be made plain: 'And a call, pure, long and throbbing. Long in dying call' denotes the sound of the blind piano-tuner's tuning-fork (p. 263)—he has already been met on p. 180 when Bloom helped him across the street. His halting return for his forgotten tuning-fork is described by repeated taps of his stick from p. 280 onwards.

Thus the whole chapter concentrates on the sounds of the bar, concert room or restaurant (adjoining rooms) of the Ormond Hotel, where many of our old acquaintances meet to drink, sing or eat. Simon Dedalus sings an aria from *Martha* (not Bloom's typist correspondent Martha!) and the applause is described in a way that only Joyce's techniques could compass:

—Bravo! Clapclap. Goodman, Simon. Clappyclapclap. Encore! Clapclipclap. Sound as a bell. Bravo, Simon. Clapclopclap. Encore, enclap, said, cried, clapped all. Ben Dollard, Lydia Douce, George Lidwell, Pat, Mina, two gentlemen with two tankards, Cowley, first gent with tank and bronze Miss Douce and gold Miss Mina.

Any passage from this incredible chapter is equally quotable; in reading it, it is possible to get so enraptured by the sheer virtuosity of the sounds and their close interconnection with the plain facts of the surroundings and the company, that it tends to be forgotten that the 'story' moves on in this chapter too.

Four o'clock is the hour of the seduction of Molly by Boylan. Bloom is in a shop making his feeble gesture of riposte by buying writing-paper for a letter to his Martha; he catches sight of Boylan as he does so:

> He eyed and saw afar on Essex bridge a gay hat riding on a jaunting car. It is. Third time. Coincidence.
>
> Jingling on supple rubbers is jaunted from the bridge to Ormond quay. Follow. Risk it. Go quick. At four. Near now. Out.
>
> —Twopence, sir, the shopgirl dared to say.
>
> —Aha ... I was forgetting ... Excuse ...
>
> And four [the 4d change from his sixpence]
>
> At four she. Winsomely she on Bloohimwhom smiled. Bloo smi qui go. Ternoon. Think you're the only pebble on the beach? Does that to all. For men.   p. 262

Boylan enters the bar and drinks a sloe-gin (less offensive on the breath than beer or whisky). Bloom accosts Richie Goulding (Stephen's uncle, p. 90) at the door of the restaurant and they go in to eat a belated lunch together, first ordering cider and beer (note that the considerate Bloom pities the old bald waiter's feet, p. 266). Then (at the bottom of p. 266):

> Jingle a tinkle jaunted.
>
> Bloom heard a jing, a little sound. He's off. Light sob of breath Bloom sighed on the silent blue-hued flowers ...

Boylan is en route for his assignation.

Bloom writes his note to Martha (pp. 278–9) amidst the singing; his thoughts modulate with the moods of the music— Molly, Milly and little lost Rudy (p. 283). The lemon soap obtrudes on p. 285, as Bloom, now somewhat flatulent ('Gassy thing that cider'), gets up to go. The chapter ends with one of the most daring sequences in the book, one of those that led Virginia Woolf to call it 'underbred', and that no doubt justified Ezra Pound in coining the phrase about Joyce's 'arsthetic obsession'. Bloom having left the restaurant sees among the junk in an antique shop window the picture of a gallant Irish patriot,

Robert Emmet, and remembers his heroic words: at the same time he is unable to resist farting; but he manages to wait (considerately) until a 'lady' acquaintance has passed him, and the clatter—'Tram. Kran, kran'— of a tramcar will disguise it. The witty way in which the noble words—'Then and not till then let my epitaph be written. I have done'—are interwoven with the external and internal rumbles of tram and Bloom's intestines, culminating in the emission of wind on the word 'Done', is a masterly example of form exactly fitting content. It is reminiscent, in a way, of Donne's equally perfect closure of his compasses' circle:

> Thy firmness draws my circle just,
> And makes me end where I begun.
>
> A VALEDICTION FORBIDDING MOURNING

The Homeric parallel, Sirens, is pretty obvious here. The two barmaids get their living by charming men into their bar to drink. The teasing trick of 'Sonnez la cloche' (ringing the bell) by smacking a garter on a plump smackable thigh is one of Miss Douce's little enticements, and characteristically it is chiefly for Blazes Boylan that she entertains the males at the bar in this way (p. 265).

As for the *Fuga per canonem*, this is merely an indication that the various strands of sound enunciated in the opening pages will repeat and interweave in the manner of counterpoint in music. Naturally there is no close formal correspondence between a canon or fugue (in which tunes follow one another or seem to fly from each other) and the verbal repetitions and minglings that are so dazzlingly performed by Joyce in this, the most successful chapter of the book, technically speaking. It repays a thousandfold the study it demands; and once the method is grasped, it is comparatively straightforward. There is no need to look for the whole musical textbook-full of contrapuntal devices, any more than it is necessary to chase up all the rhetorical tricks in the 'Aeolus' chapter.

CHAPTER XII

Homeric parallel: The Cyclops.   Art: Politics.
Time: 5 p.m.   Place: The Tavern (Barney Kiernan's).
Organ: Muscles.   Symbol: Fenian.
Technique: Gigantism.

The Cyclops was a one-eyed giant whose cave Odysseus invaded, and from whom he escaped only after a contest which ended with the hurling of a huge rock from the cliffs after the departing ships. In this chapter Homer's inhospitable one-track-minded giant becomes a bigoted patriot, a Fenian, who makes it clear that he would throw out of Ireland not merely the English invaders but also all Jews, and as Bloom decamps with his friends the Irish Cyclops throws a Jacobs' biscuit tin after him. (Jacobs were a Dublin firm of biscuit-makers.) The Homeric story is thus closely followed, and there are several correspondent details that the reader who knows his *Odyssey* can amuse himself by discovering.

The chapter is not easy, however. First of all, without any warning the narrator of the incident changes to a common Irish lower-middle-class ne'er-do-well who speaks in demotic Dublinese, with all the facetious vulgarisms of a *habitué* of the tavern. For instance, he talks of kicking the citizen's (Fenian 'giant's') dog 'where it wouldn't blind him' (p. 309). The manner is racy, humorous, exaggerated and vivid, with its own virtues as a narrative style. The reader is kept close to the scene by frequent apostrophes:

> So anyhow Terry [the barman] brought the three pints Joe was standing and begob the sight nearly left my eyes when I saw him hand out a quid. O, as true as I'm telling you. A goodlooking sovereign.   pp. 295–6

It is as if we were in the tavern listening to the narrator. We get, too, a jaundiced but accurate view of Bloom: 'So Bloom slopes in with his cod's eye on the dog' (p. 301)—which is vivid and revealing, for it indicates that Bloom, like his creator, dislikes or fears dogs, though he loves his own cat. If the chapter were left to this seedy Dublin pub-crawler who has descended to the level of a debt-collector it would be plain sailing.

But we haven't read a page before a long paragraph of legal language interrupts the racy flow. It appears to be a court order directing one Geraghty to pay his debt to a Jewish grocer in weekly instalments. What has happened is that the narrator's opening anecdote about one of the bad debts he is collecting has suddenly grown an enormous limb. This Joyce called *Gigantism;* there are to be many examples of it in this chapter, and some of them are very funny, others rather tedious. If you chose to cut out all the gigantisms you would have a clear connected account; whether you share Joyce's elaborate, even laboured, joke rests between you and your sense of humour.

It has already been shown how Joyce enjoys long lists of names such as those that Rabelais inserted into his Gargantuan stories (for instance, p. 118, at the beginning of the 'Aeolus' chapter, VII). Here are obvious parodies of, or tributes to, Rabelais, as in the description of the giant on pp. 294-5. There is a long list of names (one of several) on p. 295, and you may or may not think it funny to find among the growing list of Irish heroes of antiquity the Rose of Castille, Patrick W. Shakespeare, Brian Confucius, and Ben Howth (a headland bordering Dublin Bay); or a guest list, at the fashionable wedding of Miss Fir Conifer of Pine Valley, consisting entirely of trees—Mrs· Poll Ash and Miss O. Mimosa San (p. 325).

Not all the interspersions are gigantisms. Some are short and pithy, e.g. the four lines on p. 302, or the four lines on p. 313 amplifying the reflection in proverbial terms on Bloom:

Gob, he'd have a soft hand under a hen.

Ga Ga Gara. Klook Klook Klook. Black Liz is our hen. She lays eggs for us. When she lays her egg she is so glad. Gara. Klook Klook Klook. Then comes good uncle Leo. He puts his hand under black Liz and takes her fresh egg. Gaga ga ga Gara. Klook Klook Klook.

This is not so much a gigantism as a diminution into nursery talk.

Amid all the political talk and the stylistic virtuosities the story of Bloom's day proceeds. Joe Hynes invites the narrator for a drink, and though usually penniless pays with a gold sovereign (p. 296)—this is one he has drawn, on Bloom's encouragement, from the cashier at the newspaper office (p. 121). Bloom is hoping to meet Martin Cunningham (p. 301) about Dignam's insurance money (p. 311), but refuses all drink, being 'a prudent member'. He does, however, accept a cigar, thus echoing the burning brand with which Odysseus ground out the Cyclops' eye (p. 302). Bloom is not welcome to the chauvinistic citizen, or to the ignorant narrator, because he will not drink with them and persists in discussing in factual scientific terms whatever subject arises. The note of reasoned yet exasperating exposition in Bloom's talk, quite unsuitable to a pub discussion, is neatly orchestrated. But Bloom has again to endure talk of Boylan and Molly (p. 317) and his reactions, though described from the viewpoint of the low-class narrator, are shown to be much the same as on previous occasions. There is a beautiful example of a Freudian slip on p. 311, where Bloom talks of a wife's *admirers*, when he meant to say *advisers*.

The story of the Gold Cup winner, Throwaway, is continued. Lenehan comes in (p. 323) with 'a face on him as long as a late breakfast', and announces the 20-1 outsider's victory. When Bloom, tired of waiting in uncongenial, even hostile, company (his claim to Irish nationality had been rudely spat upon on p. 330, and his pronouncement of the doctrine of universal love spurned on p. 331) goes out in search of Cunningham, Lenehan reveals that it was Bloom who had tipped Throwaway to Bantam Lyons, and surmises that he had won at least £5 on it. This naturally enrages the narrator and the citizen, for Bloom has stood no one a drink, and his excuse for going out is transparently false—he has gone, they think, to collect his winnings (p. 333). Meantime Cunningham has come into the tavern, and when he sees that Bloom on his return is the object of vilification by the now drunken citizen, he hustles him out.

But not before a delicious piece of irony. The talk is of Jewry, and Bloom, not lacking in courage in defence of his reasoned principles, bursts out:

> —Mendelssohn was a jew and Karl Marx . . . Your God was a jew. Christ was a jew like me.
>
> Gob, the citizen made a plunge back into the shop.
>
> —By Jesus, says he, I'll brain that bloody jewman for using the holy name. By Jesus, I'll crucify him so I will. Give us that biscuitbox here. p. 340

Notice also Bloom's compassionate views and temperament throughout the chapter—e.g. his practical pity for Mrs. Dignam, and for Mrs. Breen (p. 319), whose eccentric husband the others are making heartless fun of. Bloom also thinks of the dead Rudy (p. 336), and he continues to be preoccupied with his job when on p. 322 he tackles Hynes about the 3/- debt but gives him longer to pay in return for Hynes's influence with Myles Crawford, the editor of the paper, about the puff for the Keyes advertisement.

Finally, among all the political talk there is a reference to the new (in 1904) King Edward VII that put political obstacles in the way of the publication of *Ulysses*:

> —Well, says J.J. [the barrister O'Molloy]. We have Edward the peacemaker now.
>
> —Tell that to a fool, says the citizen. There's a bloody sight more pox than pax about that boyo. Edward Guelph-Wettin! p. 329

No wonder the printers and publishers of the war years and the 1920s fought shy of the book.

CHAPTER XIII

> Homeric parallel: Nausicaa.   Art: Painting.
> Time: 8 p.m.   Place: The Rocks on Sandymount shore.
> Organs: Eye and Nose.   Symbol: Virgin.
> Technique: Tumescence and Detumescence.

Nausicaa was a beautiful princess who with her attendant maidens went down to the river to wash their clothes; while there they played with a ball which fell into deep water, and their cries woke Odysseus who was sleeping in the bushes, exhausted after being washed up naked on the shore.

These elements of the Homeric story are all present (with many more) in this chapter. But Nausicaa has become the prurient Gerty MacDowell (already mentioned on pp. 252 and 331), an avid reader of women's magazine trash, on which all her conscious thoughts are modelled. The first sentence is enough to turn the stomach of any sensitive reader: 'The summer evening had begun to fold the world in its mysterious embrace.' The sugary words match the nauseatingly false poeticism, and the reader soon realises he is being admitted to the mind of one who thinks herself 'as fair a specimen of winsome Irish girlhood as one could wish to see' (p. 346); and Gerty strives to become as winsome as the heroines of trashy romances, by following the beauty hints of 'Madame Vera Verity, directress of the Woman Beautiful page of the Princess novelette' (p. 347). She cuts her hair at the new moon, and her nails on Thursday (for wealth), and 'as a telltale flush, delicate as the faintest rosebloom, crept into her cheeks she looked so lovely in her sweet girlish shyness' because Edy Boardman, one of her companions, has suggested that she is the sweetheart of little Tommy, aged four, one of the darling twins they are looking after.

But it is soon plain that the twins are little horrors, quarrelling over a sandcastle built like a Martello tower (*cf.* Chapter I); and this should make the reader suspect that Gerty, too, is not quite the dainty Irish beauty that she pretends to be in this her interior monologue—for it is now recognisable as hers. Gerty has been hoping to ensnare Reggie Wylie (whose brother was competing in the college races on p. 236), but Reggie is still at school, and has been made by his father to stop cycling in front of her window because he has to stay in and work at his books. But Gerty is feeling jilted, and her daydreams turn towards handsome aristocratic strangers—for she soon admits that she is nearly twenty-two and in need of a husband (p. 350). It is also soon obvious, beneath the thoughts she presents to the world, that she is a nasty-minded little minx, who practises 'crying nicely before the mirror', and is rather too nice about her frilly knickers with their different sets of ribbons; it is not natural for a girl of twenty-two to crimson at the unladylike words of Cissy, who would slap Tommy 'on the beetoteetom' (p. 351). So when Bloom appears, is involved with the ball, and takes an obvious interest in her as she poses on a rock, she begins to tease him by taking off her hat to display her lovely hair, swinging her buckled shoe, and exhibiting her transparent stockings. She is fully conscious that 'she had raised the devil in him' (p. 358). This, of course, could be purely romantic novelette talk, but Gerty still has some surprises. When the end of her part of the chapter is reached (p. 365), she is shown to be lame, and a glance back over what has been read may reveal the indication that was missed: she can't kick the ball without an effort (pp. 353–4), she is jealous of Cissy's ability to run (p. 357, l. 19 and p. 363, l. 8), and she admits to one shortcoming, the result of 'an accident coming down Dalkey hill' (p. 362, l. 5). How else, it may be wondered, have we been misled by accepting Gerty at her own valuation? She is ostensibly too ladylike to acknowledge even to herself her visits to the lavatory (p. 353, ll. 11 and 19), and her thoughts are invaded now and again by the sounds of the church service in honour of the Virgin proceeding from the quiet church of Howth Abbey. Is she as virginal in thought as we are brainwashed into believing?

But Gerty knows all about male masturbation (p. 363, l. 27), and her exhibition of frilly underwear is designed to rouse Bloom; she fully realises just what she is doing, and what he is doing, with his hands in his pockets. She leans back on the rock (pp. 363–4) as the prose gets more and more tumescent, until the climax comes for Bloom with—a magical touch this—the ascent and bursting of a rocket from a firework display (at the Mirus charity bazaar that the Viceroy was on his way to open in Chapter X). The next paragraph shows beyond doubt that Gerty knew perfectly well what had been going on, and was conscious of her provocative part, and exactly what 'devil' she had roused. Joyce later removes all possibility of misunderstanding by having Bloom refer to 'That little limping devil' on p. 367, which is surely not merely a reference to the lame seductress. As she goes she waves the wad of perfumed cotton-wool that she keeps in her kerchief pocket (p. 348), and this scent, wafted slowly on the evening air, reaches Bloom some minutes later (on p. 372) and sets his mind's nose twitching. The organs of this chapter are eye and nose, and the art celebrated is painting, but there is very little painterly talk and very little more celebration of the joys of sight in this chapter than in any other. There are references to the play of light on pp. 373–4, for instance, and some mention of pavement artists (p. 355), but Joyce's eye is normally so perspicacious that these, and many others, pass for his usual manner and make no special mark. It is, however, through the eye that the sexual encounter first takes place, and then, by the medium of Gerty's cheap perfume, through the nose.

The chapter belongs to Gerty and her frilly knickers up to p. 365. (She was not to know, of course, that Bloom had an underwear fetish.) But from then till the end of the chapter we have some of the most movingly characteristic Bloomian moments of the whole book. Bloom is now exhausted, with the various duties and pleasures of a day that began thirteen hours earlier. All the memories of his day's wanderings return, whether his job of selling advertising space (pp. 373, 375 and 378), the Dignam funeral and his compassionate labours for the widow (p. 378), the *Sweets of Sin* (pp. 366 and 379), Martha Clifford and her silly letter (pp. 367 and 379) or above all, though now not so insistently, what had happened at No. 7 Eccles Street at about half-past-four, when unaccountably and ominously his watch had stopped (p. 367). These thoughts and a host of others become more and more jumbled, and increasingly difficult to follow in a logical way, as the detumescence continues, progressing from body to mind, until he finally dozes off (p. 379), 'Just for a few' (p. 380). And, fittingly in every way, it is the virgin Gerty who has the last word, as the cuckoo clock in the priest's house announces nine times that her foreign gentleman with the dark sad eyes and aristocratic mien is a cuckold.

It is easy to miss the irony of this chapter, as the reader is induced by the over-ripe prose of Gerty to think she is as bloodless and as artless as the heroines of the penny romances that are her spiritual pabulum. It is as if Joyce is showing up the falsity of the romantic view of human existence. That Gerty should be lame in her leg is hardly her fault, and our compassion ought to go out to her, as Bloom's eventually does. But there is little excuse for her wilful denial of her body, her pretence of being shocked at the two ordinary girls' language, her imagined revulsion for ordinary food, and her desire only to eat roses and violets. Whether Joyce himself is passing a harsh judgment on her is uncertain, but there is little doubt that he is at any rate condemning that sort of art, that view of life, which ignores the animal half of human nature.

Among Bloom's thoughts as he goes to sleep is the three-day labour of Mrs. Purefoy (p. 377), and he resolves to call at the hospital to enquire after her. It is this errand of mercy that occupies the next chapter. But before moving on there is one small puzzle to examine. On pp. 376–7 a beautifully written paragraph, in flowing prose of great skill, interrupts Bloom's monologue. In spite of the 'yumyum rhododendrons', the words and the observations are hardly those of Bloom. Why does Joyce insert this paragraph, the only piece of external narrative in the chapter? A. Walton Litz, in *The Art of James Joyce* (p. 30), demonstrates the care Joyce took in the composition of it. It is fascinating to see how the writer's mind worked on the improvement. But it does seem odd that just this one paragraph (and possibly the last twenty lines of the chapter) is given to neither Gerty nor Bloom. Or perhaps it does after all register a moment when Bloom rises to poetical heights usually denied to him.

CHAPTER XIV

Homeric parallel: The Oxen of the Sun.   Art: Medicine.
Time: 10 p.m.   Place: The Maternity Hospital.
Organ: The Womb.   Symbol: Mothers.
Technique: Embryonic Development.

Joyce now writes an even more confusing chapter. The events of it are quickly summarised: Bloom visits the Lying-In Hospital (p. 382, l. 25) where Mrs. Purefoy is in her third day of labour; while he is in talk with the nurse, who is an acquaintance, young Dr. Dixon, who had treated Bloom's bee-sting (p. 70), comes past and invites him into the medical students' common room (p. 384, l. 13), where enjoying a meal of sardines and beer (p. 384, l. 32) are assembled Lynch (an old friend of Stephen's from *A Portrait*), Madden, the scrounger Lenehan, a Scotsman Crotthers, Punch Costello, who is very drunk, and Stephen, who is more so (p. 386, l. 5). They spend the next hour or so arguing mainly on obstetric and gynaecological subjects (as befits the place, the art, the organ and the symbol). The thunder that had been brewing all this hot June day (p. 69) suddenly breaks out in a torrential downpour, drenching Mulligan, who was expected at the hospital, and Alex Bannon, Milly's spark (pp. 28 and 68). They join the company (p. 399) and Bannon shows snapshots of Milly (p. 401, l. 35), not realising Bloom is her father till the very end of the chapter (p. 423, l. 33). The nurse enters (p. 403, l. 7) to speak to Dixon, who is in charge of Mrs. Purefoy's case, and soon a successful delivery is announced (p. 407, l. 12), to considerable éclat among the company. Suddenly Haines, the Oxford lover of things Celtic, looks in to tell them he can't stay but will meet his friends at Westland Row station at 11.10 p.m. (p. 409, l. 23). Stephen (who still has nearly £3 left) now invites everyone to go with him to Burke's public house. Out they rush in a babel of drunken voices, and Bloom, realising that Stephen is in need of paternal care, follows, but only drinks ginger cordial to the others' beer and absinthe (p. 421, l. 38). The chapter ends in a drunken spree.

This fairly simple narrative is told in a variety of styles, beginning (after three invocations) with what appears to be a literal translation of the obscurest and dullest mediaeval Latin prose, moving on to Middle English, and so through a chronological succession of authors until the last four pages of intoxicated jabber in various comic dialects and snatches of different languages, the last being modern slangy American. Thus Joyce mirrors in language the development of the embryo in the womb; as the months of gestation succeed one another, so do the imitations (some brilliant, some pretty corny) of the greatest English—or Irish—prose writers. It is therefore a history of English prose in examples devised by the author: a remarkable piece of virtuosity, if often tiresome because hard to follow. Nor is the chronological sequence strictly kept. It appears that the development of the embryo is not uniform, but one part of the body often gains a lead over others; and Joyce exemplifies this by occasionally inserting a paragraph out of sequence. Sometimes a single word or phrase is clearly anachronistic, and Joyce must have realised this; so we can only conclude that again he was demonstrating the uneven progress of life in the womb. At the appropriate stages of the embryo's growth he also inserted references to the developing organs: at the beginning of the chapter the sardines in olive oil (p. 384) are described as headless 'fishes in an oily water', somewhat like the embryo at one month.

There are also many references to oxen, cows and bulls. Foot-and-mouth disease, for instance, is introduced when Lenehan tells Stephen he has read Mr. Deasy's letter (from p. 37, etc.) in the evening paper (p. 395). Papal bulls enter the discussion with Pope Hadrian IV ('farmer Nicholas', p. 397); and girls are described in bovine terms—'a monstrous fine bit of cowflesh' (p. 403, l. 14) or 'a skittish heifer, beef to the heel' (p. 394, l. 29). This is one of the ways in which the Homeric parallel of 'The Oxen of the Sun' works. In the *Odyssey*, the mariners land in Sicily, the three-cornered island of Trinacria, several times alluded to in the chapter, including a reference to the red triangle on a Bass bottle label (p. 411). There they defy the prohibition on the eating of the sacred oxen of the Sun, with the usual dire consequences. Page 411 is largely devoted to this episode, but it does not to me appear very significant. The Sun is of course the lifegiver, the male element in reproduction; and you can see Bloom himself in this light as he enters the feminine precincts devoted to childbirth, removing his hat (p. 383).

Bloom's kindly considerate nature is shown often to advantage, as is his prudence. He accepts the beer from the riotous young men, but 'anon full privily he voided the more part in his neighbour glass' (p. 385). He is, as usual, the essence of sweet reasonableness in argument, always bearing in mind the pain of childbirth while the others, whether medical students or not, maintain a bawdily callous masculine attitude. When they finally rush out to the pub, it is Bloom who stays behind long enough to send a message of congratulation and sympathy to the exhausted mother (p. 420). And he again looks with compassion on the reckless Stephen, in a wonderfully expressive pastiche of Malory on p. 388. Particularly admirable is the paragraph on p. 383 in which he ingratiates himself with Nurse Callan by saying he had not recognised her in the street, her face was so young (ll. 5–9). He is indeed 'the kindest that ever laid husbandly hand under hen' (p. 385).

The Gold Cup race is described by the medical student Madden (p. 412), who had backed Sceptre because it was ridden by one O. Madden; the cream of all this long Throwaway joke is, of course, that poor Bloom is quite oblivious of having tipped Throwaway in the first place, and indeed has no interest in horses and is far too prudent to waste money on betting.

This is not the most interesting of the chapters, since a good deal of it is devoted to discussion of remote subjects, philosophical, theosophical or medical. Their abstruseness is not made less opaque by the long series of pastiches, some of which employ extremely contorted prose, particularly in the pre-18th-century examples. It is not possible, I feel, to give a completely accurate list of the authors imitated; but here is a rough guide for those who (unlike me) think it necessary to their enjoyment of the book.

After the three triple invocations (the last of which is supposed to be the midwife's cry of triumph), we have chaotic mediaeval Latin (to p. 382). Then Middle English (or perhaps mock Anglo-Saxon), followed by Mandeville (p. 384), Malory (p. 385), a quite amusing piece of Sir Thomas Browne (pp. 390–1) with an excerpt from the Catholic liturgy. Then come Bunyan (p. 392), Pepys or Evelyn, or both (p. 394), Defoe (p. 395), Swift (p. 396), Addison and Steele (p. 399), Sterne (p. 401), Goldsmith (p. 403), Burke (p. 405), Gibbon (p. 407), nondescript medical prose of the 19th century (p. 408), Horace Walpole's Gothick style (p. 409), Lamb (p. 410), De Quincey (p. 411), Landor (p. 413), Macaulay (p. 414), more scientific English (p. 416), Newman (p. 418), Pater, Ruskin and Carlyle (p. 419), and then the torrent of polyglot drunken jabber ending with the horrible hot-gospelling harangue of Alexander J. Christ Dowie, otherwise known as Elijah, coming like any American evangelist, or the US marines in the war films, to save the world from itself. [The tone of Joyce is completely anti-American here.]

One's final judgment on this tremendously skilful chapter (I have not room to point out the dozens of references and cross-references embodied in the text) must be somewhat coloured by the amount of pleasure one gets from sheer verbal fireworks. True, our growing knowledge of Bloom deepens our respect for him, and it is interesting to see other characters such as Lenehan and Mulligan in different surroundings, always behaving characteristically; and it is in this chapter that Ulysses-Bloom finally meets Telemachus-Stephen. But the often laboured (though admittedly sometimes very funny) pastiches are, I cannot help feeling, a clumsy way of proceeding.

CHAPTER XV

Homeric parallel: Circe   Art: Magic.
Time: Midnight.   Place: The Brothel in Night-town.
Organ: Locomotor Apparatus.   Symbol: Whore.
Technique: Hallucination.

With a prospectus such as that above, we can expect this chapter to be even more difficult, less conventional, than any we have met so far. Circe was the enchantress who turned men into beasts of various kinds according to their natures, and Odysseus' men into swine. He escaped by carrying a charmed plant (moly, which has not been identified). Midnight is the hour when graves yield up their dead, the right hour for black magic; it is also the time when brothels and whores would be busiest. The whole chapter is one long series of hallucinations, and emphasis is laid on the locomotor apparatus, those parts of the body that enable man to move about.

By this point in *Ulysses* we know pretty well all there is to be known about Bloom's—and Stephen's—conscious mind. Now we delve into the subconscious. The secret desires of Bloom, the perversions that lurk just below the surface, but which have occasionally poked their heads into full consciousness during the day, are now given free rein, as in dreams. The fathers of this chapter are Freud and Sacher-Masoch. Bloom's obsession with underwear has already been established; how annoyed he was with the pug-nosed tramcar that robbed him of the sight of the rich lady's stockings (pp. 76 and 366). Now on p. 429 he is nearly run down by a tram, which reminds him of the intervening tram of the morning; and later, one of his hallucinations (pp. 447–50) consists of three rich ladies who accuse him of writing them indecent letters, and who proceed—like the Sacher-Masoch heroine, Venus in Furs, and the Fair Tyrants of James Lovebirch (p. 235)—to flourish their whips and smack their hunting-crops against their jackboots. Bloom's craving for humiliation emerges even more strongly when Bella Cohen, the madam of the whorehouse, becomes masculine Bello and treats the now feminine Bloom to the nastiest indignities (pp. 485–96), or when he is allowed by Boylan to look through the bedroom-door keyhole in No. 7 Eccles Street (p. 507). (It is interesting to note that Lenehan plays briefly the same role to Boylan as he did to the unspeakable Corley in that most unpleasant story 'Two Gallants' in *Dubliners*.) Bloom's memories and daydreams are enacted, too. He remembers his father and mother, his old flame Mrs. Breen, and episodes in his younger days and previous occupations (for he has wandered through many walks of life); and he becomes Lord Mayor of Dublin and instigator of the New Bloomusalem.

As in dreams, cakes of soap take on personality, kisses fly around like birds, fans talk and yewtrees whisper: even the End of the World speaks in a Scottish accent. Dozens of characters appear, nearly all of whose names we have met casually or significantly in the course of the book. Casual actions assume cosmic importance: when Bloom becomes the Messiah, for instance (p. 465), he eclipses the sun by extending his little finger, as he did in reality on p. 166. And of course there are hundreds of references to animals, and many different methods of moving about, in accordance with the Homeric parallel and the parts of the body celebrated.

Similar revelations of Stephen's mind are made. These are obvious enough once you have the hang of the chapter: his mother's death, his being caned at school, his love of abstruse knowledge, his argumentative style, his obsession with Shakespeare. Most clearly of all are revealed the depth of his pacifism, his Blakeian dislike of temporal and spiritual authority and his firm belief, shared by Bloom, of the need for universal love to counteract the brutality of aggression. William Blake got into trouble with the authorities for the treasonable words he uttered to a provocative begging soldier; and Stephen is knocked down by a foulmouthed English tommy, Private Carr (in real life a clerk in the British Consulate in Zürich, with whom Joyce had quarrelled), to be finally rescued by his new father Bloom, who has been looking after him ever since the drunken sortie to Burke's pub in Chapter XIV.

The chapter takes dramatic form—that is to say, it consists of stage directions and speeches. Joyce manages to convey the bewildering phantasmagoria of hallucinations and dreams by perpetually shifting the 'scenery' and transforming the dramatis personae. It is impossible to imagine this being successfully done in conventional narrative or even by interior monologue. The 'story' proceeds, too. It is not easy to distinguish the 'real' events from the hallucinations, though Joyce as usual based the chapter on real Dublin places and people. It is fitting that Circe's palace, where men became beasts, should be represented by Dublin Night-town, the brothel area; in reality this was Montague Street, called 'Monto' in popular parlance; that it deserved its reputation as the worst slum in Europe is demonstrated in the stage directions of the first few pages.

The 'real' events of the chapter, and of the intervening hour since Stephen's drunken party left Burke's, are gradually revealed, though inextricably bound up with the hallucinations. It appears that the party has split up on Westland Row station (p. 439), only Lynch accompanying Stephen to Night-town. Bloom, still paternally longing for Stephen, follows him and Lynch into the area which he has entered holding aloft his ashplant and chanting an *introit* (p. 427). Bloom is nearly run down by a sand-strewing tram (p. 429), fears unnecessarily that he has had his pocket picked by Jacky and Tommy Caffrey (p. 430)—last seen in the 'Nausicaa' chapter (p. 344). Bloom has in his pockets the lemon soap, an old potato that his grandmother gave him as a charm against the rheumatism (this is the counterpart of Odysseus' moly) and a pig's and a sheep's trotter that he has prudently bought in case of hunger in the 'wildgoosechase' he has embarked on. He gives the cooked feet to a dog which might be the Garryowen of the Citizen (p. 440).

Bloom tracks the two young men down to a superior brothel where Zoe (p. 454) entices him in (p. 469). In the music room (p. 470) are two more whores, Kitty and Florry, with Stephen playing the pianola with two fingers, and Lynch. There is some conversation and larking (e.g. p. 475), Bloom offers chocolate to Zoe (p. 484), Bella Cohen, the whoremistress, enters (p. 485), and Stephen pays her two pounds for three girls. Bloom prudently takes ten shillings (50p) back as change, and persuades Stephen to hand over to him the rest of his money (one pound six shillings and eleven pence (£1.35)), and more conversation takes place, amusingly told on pp. 502–5, a short realistic passage. Lynch pays two pence for the pianola to be activated, and they dance (p. 512) to the tune of 'My Girl's a Yorkshire Girl', last heard by the viceregal procession on p. 253. Finally the drunken Stephen raises his ashplant in both hands, smashes the gas chandelier, and rushes out (p. 517) leaving Bloom to pay a shilling for the damage (Belle had demanded ten). A row brews outside, Stephen getting into a very funny argument with the two English tommies (pp. 520–1). Bloom tries to calm them down and lead Stephen away, but in his fuddled state he manages to insult Cissy Caffrey, Private Carr's girl, and also King Edward VII. Carr knocks Stephen down (p. 528) as the police arrive. Corny Kelleher (whom we had glimpsed on p. 518 and had probably thought a phantom) at Bloom's intercession smooths things over with the officers. Meanwhile Lynch has vanished with Kitty to get Stephen's ten shillings' worth elsewhere (p. 527). Bloom, in one of the few touching moments in the book, bends over the prostrate Stephen, calls him by name, hears him murmur broken verses, and himself is moved to speak poetic phrases about the ebb and flow of the tide, as befits a mariner. As he stands guard over the helpless Stephen the final hallucination manifests itself in the form of a fairy boy of eleven, in an Eton collar; it is the eleven-years-dead eleven-day-lived Rudy, a white lambkin peeping out of his waistcoat pocket. This represents the lambs-wool 'corselet' that Molly had knitted for him—'lest he lie akeled' (p. 388). So the three protagonists of the book are brought together—Bloom, Molly and Stephen—in a moment of love. This unheroic Penelope wove no tapestry but a winding-sheet for her only son; with his death innocence fled.

With the end of the second part of 'this chaffering all-including most farraginous chronicle' (p. 420, l. 16), the wanderings of the storm-tossed Odysseus come to a pause. There is a moment of stasis before with Telemachus he turns towards home.

Puzzling and extravagant as this chapter is, in it all the themes, incidents, persons, objects and thoughts of the book are brought miraculously together. Like life, some parts of it are very funny, some disgusting, but all are fascinating. It is hard to imagine how Joyce can proceed from here. To many readers the next two chapters are arid deserts, before the final amazingly satisfying Molly Bloom monologue.

CHAPTER XVI

> Homeric parallel: Eumaeus.   Art: Navigation.
> Time: 1 a.m.   Place: The Cabman's Shelter.
> Organ: The Nerves.   Symbol: Sailors.
> Technique: Narrative (old).

Notice the heading III on p. 533. The last section of *Ulysses* now begins, mirroring the *Nostos*, the return home, of Odysseus. The three chapters remaining also mirror the three chapters of the *Telemachia*, Section I, in their technique: Chapter I employed 'young narrative', Chapter II 'personal catechism', Chapter III 'male monologue'; while now come 'old narrative', 'impersonal catechism' and 'female monologue'.

The Homeric parallel, the symbol and the art are easily recognisable: Odysseus and Telemachus come disguised to the hut of Eumaeus, a swineherd who feeds them, not recognising his king and master; Bloom and Stephen are provided with undrinkable coffee and an uneatable bun in one of the Temperance shelters erected for cabmen and others compelled to be away from home late at night. A drunken yarning sailor, from the barque *Rosevean* that Stephen saw entering the Liffey at 11 a.m. (p. 56, also p. 249) is there too, the chief example of the chapter's ruling symbol, and himself a minor Odysseus; and the shelter is full of jarvies, the cabmen who navigate the streets of Dublin. There are many references to ships and sailors in the chapter.

The organ celebrated in this chapter is supposed to be the Nerves. As far as I can see, there is little meaningful reference to the nerves, of any sort—in fact, the chapter is particularly enervated, lacking in nervous energy. Perhaps this is one of Joyce's jokes—or this reader is not too bright.

But the striking feature is the technique—'old narrative'. 'Old' must be taken to mean 'tired, lassitudinous'; or possibly it merely denotes the style—the as it were spoken style—of middle-aged Bloom, as opposed to the lively, literary, imaginative, flickering style of young Stephen's mind in Chapter I. Every sentence is an inanimate agglomeration of dead metaphors, clichés, the flatfooted worthy mouthings of a small town councillor, a grocer aspiring to politics, a businessman with little education trying to impress a committee. The first words are symptomatic: 'preparatory to anything else' for 'first'; 'the greater bulk', a pleonasm; 'generally', a useless word; 'orthodox samaritan fashion', a coy Biblical reference; 'which he very badly needed', a clause not properly tied in to the meaning of the sentence, and in any case almost superfluous. Joyce manages to keep this up for nearly the whole chapter of fifty-three pages, yet we are compelled to read on with a horrible feeling of inevitability; perhaps it is *our* nerves that are being played upon. Not only is the style tired and old, but the narrative seems at times to lose itself, subjecting itself to corrections—as on p. 537, l. 10, where it goes back to correct a totally unimportant detail of twelve lines back.

Is it some new narrator, as in the 'Cyclops' chapter (XII)? My own view is that it is the speaking voice of Bloom himself—not the interior monologue, the gallimaufry of sensations, that presents the true man, but Bloom trying, like a humble lay preacher, to show up well in conversation with a brilliant young scholar whom he admires and would ingratiate himself with.

When Bloom's words are reported directly they do not differ in style from the flatulent narrative:

> —Now touching a cup of coffee . . . it occurs to me you ought to sample something in the shape of solid food, say a roll of some description.
> p. 542

These are the words of a man who will say 'commence' instead of 'begin', who drinks 'Adam's ale' when others are content with 'water'.

For it is by now obvious that Bloom is only half-educated. Part of the fun of the chapter is that he often fails to grasp Stephen's meaning. When they discuss the existence of the soul, Stephen refers to the doctrine that it is incorruptible because it is a simple substance (as Donne said, 'Whatever dies was not mixt equally'); Bloom takes him to be talking about 'simple souls', a colloquialism for humble or primitive people (pp. 554 and 557). Bloom is at his most foolish in the final conversation about music, beginning on p. 581. He takes the word 'protestant' (in the well-known ballad setting of words of Lovelace) to have primarily a sectarian significance, he thinks Meyerbeer wrote the *Seven Last Words on the Cross*, that Mendelssohn represents the severe classical school and that *Don Giovanni* is a light opera. Best of all, he wonders whether John Bull, the Elizabethan polyphonic composer, is 'the political celebrity of that ilk'.

Some commentators excuse Bloom on the grounds of his utter exhaustion; but I think that Joyce is making sure that we do not elevate this very ordinary man into a too heroic figure. He is, it is true, devoid of strong emotion at this dead hour; he has almost forgotten Boylan (there is a direct reference on p. 539 and two veiled ones on pp. 547, l. 36 and 567, l. 37), and is able to produce Molly's photograph in an attempt to entice Stephen to his home. (Here Bloom again is reminiscent of Richard Rowan in *Exiles*.) Most of his usual obsessions appear somewhere in the chapter, and there are many references to the day's events and thoughts: Throwaway, p. 568, Menton's hat (pp. 117 and 575), his argument with the Citizen (pp. 563–4), underwear, particularly rumpled stockings (pp. 165, 370 and 558), and so on.

The cliché-ridden style exactly renders the fatigue, the exhaustion of passion, and all that is left is Bloom's pedestrian, maddeningly reasonable, arithmetical mind, neatly featured by Joyce in his favourite word 'phenomenon' (p. 554, for instance), that so enraged the Irish narrator of Chapter XII.

Stephen says little; he is recovering from an almighty bender, and at first shows no animation. He is in a state when it is easier to be unwillingly led than to resist; he cannot even say a convincing no to the repulsive coffee, and spasmodically attempts to respond to the overtures of this helpful stranger who has a solemn line in talk. The flatness of his mind is neatly revealed on p. 565, ll. 8–16, one of the very few passages that are his own. He goes along with Bloom not because he is attracted to him or by his talk of music lessons, Italian duets, concert tours or Molly's charms, but merely because he has not yet the will to resist, to become himself again. In fact he finds Bloom slightly repulsive (p. 581, l. 15).

There are, however, several very funny passages, the fun even breaking through the encrustation of the lifeless verbiage. (I myself find the protracted joke of the style rather tedious.) The sailor's long yarns, especially the egg-shooting prowess of 'Simon Dedalus', are very amusing. So is Hynes's paragraph in the newspaper describing the Dignam funeral, where poor Bloom, who put in everyone else's name, including Stephen's and McCoy's, who weren't there, and Mackintosh, the mysterious figure of the book, finds his own name ludicrously misspelt 'L. Boom' (p. 568). A further irony is added to the Throwaway story when on p. 569 Bloom thinks that Bantam Lyons had backed the French horse Maximum II, not even Sceptre. There is also some wry amusement to be had in watching Bloom's calculation of the money he has wasted on this pursuit of Stephen, and his consoling reflection that he might yet be amply repaid (p. 567). Joyce sometimes admits a joke that is outside the frame of reference of the chapter's 'old narrative', as in the final picture of the horse's miring (p. 585).

Two of the book's themes that make their point in this chapter are usurpers (the Tichborne claimant emphasises this on p. 570) and Irish nationalism, not only in the references to Parnell and Kitty O'Shea, the unfaithful wife (see p. 144), but throughout the chapter in the person of Skin-the-goat, the attendant at the shelter, who played a prominent part in the Phoenix Park murder of the English diplomat, and who has been referred to several times in the course of the book.

But on the whole the chapter is sparing in its looking before and after. The general effect, not only in language but in subject-matter and narrowness of reference, is entirely aippropriate to the exhaustion of one o'clock in the mornng. I wonder, however, if Joyce bored himself with the deadness of it. Contrast these first two sentences from Chapter I, 'young narrative':

> Stately, plump Buck Mulligan came from the stairhead, bearing a bowl of lather on which a mirror and a razor lay crossed. A yellow dressing-gown, ungirdled, was sustained gently behind him by the mild morning air.

What a long way we have travelled from that spare, direct, pointed diction, that careful selection of significant detail, that euphonious rise and fall of the living voice!

CHAPTER XVII

> Homeric parallel: Ithaca.   Art: Science.
> Time: 2 a.m.   Place: Bloom's House.
> Organ: Skeleton.   Symbol: Comets.
> Technique: Catechism (impersonal).

Without warning, another chapter begins in a bizarre manner. The technique is the impersonal catechism of the scientific enquirer; the searching questions, even when probing into personal foibles or secrets, demand factual, statistical, quantifiable answers. Human emotion is not so much rejected as utterly ignored; the human body is reduced to its skeleton. Comets (no in fact noticeable in the chapter) are all tail.

Odysseus returns disguised as a humble serving-man to his palace in Ithaca; Bloom has to scale the area railings and let himself in by the kitchen door, having left his keys in the pocket of his everyday trousers when he put on his black suit for Dignam's funeral (p. 59). Odysseus and Telemachus together killed or routed all the suitors, and Bloom seems to assert himself rather more than usual as he recounts his day's adventures, with suitable omissions, to Molly (he even asks for his breakfast in bed the next morning, as we learn in the first lines of the next chapter, p. 659). Yet his dominant mood, as he finally gets himself into his desecrated bed, first removing crumbs and flakes of the potted meat Boylan had sent with the fruit (pp. 226 and 652), is of resignation and abnegation. He reflects:

> That each one who enters imagines himself to be the first to enter whereas he is always the last term of a preceding series even if the first term of a succeeding one, each imagining himself to be first, last, only and alone, whereas he is neither first nor last nor only nor alone in a series originating in and repeated to infinity. p. 652

He sees no point in confronting Boylan or arranging for divorce (p. 654), consoling himself partly by his recognition of 'the futility of triumph or protest or vindication' and of 'the apathy of the stars', and partly by realising that he can still kiss 'the plump mellow yellow smellow melons of [Molly's] rump'.

Before we reach this ceremony of homecoming and the magical going to sleep of the Wanderer, we are led through the long series of question and answer of which Joyce was apparently inordinately proud. The events narrated are all minor ones: Stephen and Bloom, in amicable discussion of a variety of subjects (pp. 586–8), arrive at No. 7 Eccles Street; Bloom lets Stephen in by the hall door (p. 590), lights the kitchen fire (reminding Stephen of the English Dean of Studies in *A Portrait*, p. 184), vainly offers Stephen a wash with the lemon soap (p. 593), understands at last the whole Throwaway incident (p.

596), makes cocoa (p. 597), remembers other previous links with Stephen (p. 600), discusses Hebrew and old Irish, hears Stephen sing the anti-semitic ballad *Hugh of Lincoln* (p. 611), offers Stephen lodgings and returns his money (p. 616), arranges for Stephen to give Italian lessons to Molly (that *voglio* question (p. 66) would at last be settled!) and take singing lessons from her, and to meet him for walks and talks (p. 617), lets Stephen out (p. 619), and joins him in urinating in the garden (p. 623). Bloom, now alone, bangs his head on some re-arranged furniture in the front parlour (p. 626), lights a cone of incense (p. 628), begins to undress (p. 631), daydreams of his country estate (see p. 70), and of making a fortune to buy it with (p. 638), unlocks what he thought were private drawers to peruse private papers and talismans (pp. 642 and 644), meditates on his ancestry and dreams of long journeys (pp. 645–8), broods on his day (pp. 649–50), undresses and gets into bed (p. 652). Lying with his head at his wife's feet (an odd way for them to sleep), he sinks to rest in the posture of a child in the womb, beside Molly, who is now likened to Gea-Tellus, the primordial earth-mother of mankind (p. 658). The insistent questions cease to elicit rational responses, and the last one of all leaves us in no place.

Many of Bloom's preoccupations naturally recur in this ostensibly 'scientific', factual chapter. There is a good deal of play with the physical circumstances of his daily life, his home and his youth. The contents of his library and the items of his day's expenditure are enumerated with as little warmth as the exact route of the journey home and the details of the water supply of the City of Dublin. But it would be wrong to say that there is no poetry; when the two men go out into the back garden they are *confronted* (Joyce's word) by 'The heaventree of stars hung with humid nightblue fruit'—hardly a scientific description of the phenomena that Bloom proceeds to astronomise over (p. 619). The description of Molly's melonous bottom (quoted above, p. 122) is not couched in any terms other than emotional or imaginative ones. We should therefore be on our guard against the pretensions of science to explain everything. And the last responses elicited by the cold catechiser are not the precise geographical location of the matrimonial bed (p. 657), but elements of myth and dream, Gea-Tellus and Sinbad the Sailor and Darkinbad the Brightdayler.

Stephen's part in this chapter is subsidiary. He gradually comes back to his intelligent self, making little, no doubt, of Bloom's scientific talk. He does not allow himself to be gathered into Bloom's and Molly's domesticity: it is not in the nature of a wild goose to seek a permanent nest. He who rejects family, church and country will not commit himself to a man of such ordinariness as the prudent moralist. Nor does he show any interest in the boasted charms of Molly. But there is some promise of further contact with the pair, and it may be that Stephen will settle for a short while under the steadying influence of one who knows what it is to be an alien.

When we reach this stage in the modern *Odyssey* we realise, I think, that it is unwise to press the analogy too far. Bloom is not completely explained by Odysseus, nor Stephen by Telemachus; the Homeric story is in fact no more than a guideline, no more substantial than the piece of string that the mason uses to keep his courses level. Joyce, in erasing from the published book the Homeric titles under which he had constantly referred to the chapters in conversation and correspondence, is deliberately throwing the old story away, as the mason removes his line when the building stands complete.

CHAPTER XVIII

Homeric parallel: Penelope.　　Art:
Time:　　　　　　Place: The Bed.　　Organ: Flesh.
Symbol: Earth.　　Technique: Monologue (female).

But the book, though perhaps finished in regard to the Father and Son, Odysseus and Telemachus, has still not described the complete human condition. Half the human race is female, and so far Molly has been seen only in glimpses through the eyes of others. Bloom has constantly been preoccupied with her, and with other women's troubles, throughout the day; and more than one man thinks Molly is 'a gamey mare and no mistake' (p. 234). Now we are to be in her mind and her bed, after her returning husband has awakened her with the promise of Stephen and his own unprecedented demand for breakfast in bed. Her thoughts are set down in eight paragraphs, each without any sort of punctuation, not even 's to denote the possessive case. (In the French translation even the accents were omitted.) I use the word *thoughts*; but we are nearer here to the 'stream of consciousness' than anywhere in the book, and consciousness is not composed of thoughts nor transmissible in words, though until the secret of telepathy is discovered, mankind will have to make do with them.

After all the celebration of the various organs, Kidney, Brains, Womb, Nerves, Skeleton, Muscles, the attention is now concentrated on that part or aspect of the body that makes it desirable. Nobody will adore a woman's Lungs. After the navigation o the city, its pubs, library, hospital, brothels, we reach the intimate warmth of the bed, where we spend a third of our lives, where we begin and where we end. After all the exploration of Politics, Theology, Science, Magic, reference is made to no branch of knowledge, to no art other than the art of being desirable, or accepting bestial man as he is, of saying yes to life. Joyce placed this episode in no hour of his day, for though its clock hour and its calendar date can be deduced, it treats of timeless things.

The symbol 'Earth' connects Molly with Gea-Tellus (Greek and Latin for earth), our mother-earth, the earth-goddess, or the feminine principle of creation; and Penelope is, of course, the wife of Odysseus, faithful to him for ten years while he fights at Troy, then for ten more as he wanders the seas. As Odysseus on returning routs the suitors, so in Molly's thoughts Bloom finally supplants Boylan, who is characterised as a bounder, uncaringly taking his own pleasure (p. 663). By his side Poldy, in spite of his faults, is a considerate husband—he always wipes his feet on the mat, and he takes his hat off to Molly when he meets her in the street (p. 665). You will be continually confused as you read, for Molly's thoughts switch from Boylan to Bloom, to other men and back again in the course of a couple of lines; she does not always put proper nouns to her verbs, and 'he' can mean anybody. There is no doubt, however, that at the end it is of Bloom she is thinking when, after recalling her first sexual experiences with Lieutenant Mulvey on Gibraltar Rock, she re-enacts her acceptance of her feminine role in life and her surrender to Bloom, the one she loves best, if she can indeed *love* anybody. There is no room for romantic love in the cult of Gea-Tellus. The Earth Mother needs man to breed from, and Molly reviews many men in her monologue. It is to Life rather than to Bloom (though also to him) that she says 'Yes I will Yes'. Joyce was pleased to agree when his French translator, Benoîst-Méchin, added a final '*oui*' to his version of the original ending 'I will', 'It must end with the most positive word in the human language'. So he added 'Yes' to the English version.

It is tempting to rhapsodise over these forty-five astonishing pages; but what the reader must do is read them at one go, if he can, and savour the complete honesty of them. Unlike Gerty MacDowell, Molly admits into the consciousness the messy facts of her body. Only two 'events' occur: a train is heard whistling (pp. 675 and 683) as Molly breaks wind; and Molly, rising to use the chamber pot (there were no bathrooms in ordinary houses in those days), realises she is menstruating (p. 690). Her blood is a positive sign; for though she expects to give her favours to Boylan again, and thinks of Stephen as a possible young lover (p. 696), it is better that there should still be a chance of her bearing a real son to Bloom; and his request for two eggs with his breakfast in bed, taken in conjunction with her final 'Yes', may very well mean that the pair will resume marital relations. For this to be possible her womb must have rejected the usurper's seed.

Joyce does not tell us how many lovers—in the technical sense—Molly has had. Several men pass through her mind, some of whom could have enjoyed her, but some of whom quite obviously could not. The series of occupants of Molly's bed which Bloom gives in answer to the statistical question on p. 652 is equally misleading. Father Bernard Corrigan, for instance, was Molly's confessor (p. 662); and John Henry Menton, the solicitor, made no headway with her (p. 660). But Bartell D'Arcy the tenor (*Dubliners*, p. 195) seems to have done rather more on the choir stairs than kiss her (p. 666). A close examination of the evidence reveals only Boylan as a certain lover and D'Arcy as a possible one. Molly may be 'gamey' but is not promiscuous.

The reader is thus left with a picture of an earthy, unintellectual, ordinary woman. I don't see how any man can adequately assess the degree of truth in the portrayal. Joyce's excursion into feminine psychology must rely for its ultimate authenticity on his knowledge of man's nature rather than woman's. Nevertheless, the impression, deepening with each reading, is of naked reality. The whole book seems to be summed up in this last chapter. Not only are events of the day mentioned (Boylan (p. 671) had lost money on Sceptre—thus explaining the torn betting tickets of p. 596), but most of the book's recurrent words, symbols, themes and personalities make their final appearance. The interested reader might find amusement in counting the number of references to flowers—Blooms—in the last two pages—and in listing the nouns: music, keys, milk, sea, waves, cattle, rivers, lakes, God, atheists, priest, hell, universe, sun, rhododendrons, hat, mouth, cake, kiss, mountain, body, sky, sailors, birds, sentry, governor, girls, shawls, combs, auctions, Greeks, Jews, Arabs, Europe, market, donkeys, wheels, carts, bulls, castle, kings, shop, lover, iron, boat, lamp, torrent, fire, sunset, figtrees, gardens, streets, houses, Gibraltar, hair, wall, breasts, heart.

When you take into account the total scheme of the book, its various arts, organs of the body, symbols, Homeric references, its breadth of allusion to theology, theosophy, astronomy, literature (the dozens of quotations from Shakespeare), its rhetorical devices, its various styles (especially in Chapter XIV), its details of Dublin streets and Dublin life, its numerous personages, brought to individual life in few words (Ben Dollard 'all arse and pockets', for instance), you will recognise that it is an 'all-including chronicle'. Naturally, one reading will not unlock all its secrets. There are parts of the book that remain unexplained, in spite of a flourishing Joyce industry in the Universities; there is plenty of room for disagreement among the commentators. But *Ulysses* remains a magnificent creation; it shares with the best novels of Jane Austen that quality of being able to be read with keen delight on any page chosen at random. As with *Emma*, the 'story' does not matter. Joyce's great discovery, says Richard Ellmann, is that the ordinary is extraordinary.

7

Finnegans Wake

Ulysses was published in 1922, on Joyce's fortieth birthday. A year later he began the actual writing of *Finnegans Wake*, a task which occupied him until 1938. It is a large book of over 600 pages, and very few people have read it; fewer still have understood it: in fact, only Joyce knew the origin of multi-lingual references that go to make up each punning, puzzling sentence; and, as was hinted on p. 16, even his closest friends and most ardent supporters thought he had gone too far in a direction where no one could possibly follow him.

This is best illustrated, however, from the book itself. This is how it starts:

> riverrun, past Eve and Adam's, from swerve of shore to bend of
> bay, brings us by a commodius vicus of recirculation back to
> Howth Castle and Environs   FW 3

It is clear that this half-sentence is loaded with significance, but not at all clear what the significance is. To explain it fully would occupy several pages of this book and demand a large fund of general and specific knowledge in the reader.

Ostensibly, it describes Dublin Bay (where else would the exiled Joyce's heart be?), where the River Liffey flows out, past Adam and Eve's Church, along the southern curve of the coast (past Vico Road) and back again along the northern shore where the Hill of Howth stands sheltering the Castle. Three words here are obviously coinings. *riverrun* offers no problem. *Vicus* makes sense only to those who recognise the Neapolitan philosopher Gianbattista Vico (1688–1744), who propounded a cyclic view of history, in which four stages of development

129

succeed one another in an endless chain of events, repeating the sequence from everlasting to everlasting; similarly, as well as circling the bay, the river endlessly flows into the sea and back again, either on the rising tide or in rainclouds. *commodius* means commodious, convenient, useful, profitable, beneficial, but the misspelling draws our attention to the commode, with its chamber pot, which reminds us at once of Molly Bloom at the end of *Ulysses*, and the flow of both water and blood, the blood of life.

We might also remember that *Ulysses* began with a view of Dublin Bay and a comparison of it to a shaving bowl and also to a bowl of vomit: 'The ring of bay and skyline held a dull green mass of liquid'—'a bowl of bitter waters.' 'Warm sunshine merrying over the sea. The nickel shavingbowl shone, forgotten, on the parapet.'

But this is only the uppermost layer of meaning. Among many pronouncements about his work that he uttered to his friends as the book was composing, he said, 'Time and the river and the mountain are the real heroes of my book.' Here in the first word is the river, the Anna Liffey, which becomes in this book Anna Livia Plurabelle, the eternal universal feminine principle, yet at the same time the mortal heroine of *Finnegans Wake*, wife of the Chapelizod innkeeper whose dream constitutes the whole shifting, fantastic cycle that Joyce chooses to begin in this way and at this point. The river is also the river of time, which flowed *past Eve and Adam's* in the garden of Eden, at the beginning of man's existence. So right at the start it is stated that the book will present a view of all human history, recurring in its cycles as the river flows into the sea from the mountain, *Howth Castle and Environs*.

The observant reader may then ask why *Environs* has a capital E. This is because the initials H C E stand for Humphrey Chimpden Earwicker, the father-figure and innkeeper, and they are to recur again and again. For HCE is Here Comes Everybody, and Haveth Childers Everywhere. He is present on p. 4—'Haroun Childeric Eggeberth', and p. 7— '*Hic cubat edilis*'.

(With the last bit of Latin Joyce also adds '*Apud libertinam parvulam*', A.L.P., Anna Livia Plurabelle, that river that is inseparable from its mountain or *alp*.)

The curious reader may then wonder how the book ends. If you turn to the last page, you read:

A way a lone a last a loved a long the

These final words lead us immediately back to the beginning. The cycle begins again, the ends are joined.

In truth, then, as Joyce himself says on p. 20, 'So you need hardly spell me how every word will be bound over to carry three score and ten toptypsical readings throughout the book of Doublends Jined.'

No one can hope to catch all the 'three-score and ten' references that each word carries, unless he is equipped with the very same mind that Joyce had. It would obviously occupy a whole lifetime to disentangle them all. No wonder Harriet Weaver, Joyce's devoted backer and benefactor, said she was grateful for the set of notes that he sent her for the first few lines of the first draft of the opening section, in 1926. It is essential that the would-be reader should realise what he is up against. It is therefore expedient to accept Joyce's help with some of the more obscure or far-flung allusions:

ll. 4–9: Sir Amory Tristram was the first Earl of Howth, who changed his name to Saint Lawrence. He had been born in North Armorica, or Brittany: and in North America a Dubliner named Sawyer had founded a new Dublin in Laurens County, Georgia, on the banks of the river Oconee; its motto was 'Doubling all the time'. Tristram was also the legendary hero who was the violator of the marriage of Iseult (Isolde) with King Mark of Cornwall. The Dublin suburb of Chapelizod takes its name from Isolde, who lived there, and it is also here that Earwicker keeps his pub, living with his wife Anna Livia, his two sons Shem and Shaun (James and John), and his daughter Issy, short for Isabel (Isolde plus Plurabelle).

l. 7: *exaggerated* is used in its original Latin sense of to mound up, *exaggerare*.

Themselse = 'another dublin 5000 inhabitants', says Joyce.

ll. 5–6: *scraggy isthmus* refers punningly to the Isthmus of Sutton, a

thin neck of land near Howth Head. We are to think of scrag of
mutton, the neck of the carcase.

ll. 4–5: *passencore* = *pas encore* (French) not yet; but also a reference
to Vico's historical cycle which would come to *pass* again.

l. 6: *wielderfight* derives from *wield* (a weapon), and *wieder*, German
for *again*. Sir Tristram would some day return, rearrive, to
re-enact his old *penisolate* (penis, Isolde, peninsular, pen in isolation) war with King Mark, which at the beginning of the book
he has not yet begun. Cornwall is a peninsula.

These cryptic allusions require much thought, and one wonders where to stop. How many languages does one need to be
conversant with? For instance *rory* (l. 13) combines the Erse
word for red and the Latin *róridus*, dewy. *mishe* (l. 9) comes from
the Erse 'I am', meaning 'I am a Christian', words which the
convert will say when he is baptised—*tauf* is the German for
baptise. *regginbrow* (l. 14) is akin to the German word for
rainbow, *regenbogen*, and *ringsome* to *ringsum*, around; and
Howth, says Joyce, is akin to the Danish word for head, *hoved*.

And how many layers of meaning can be uncovered? Take
the apparently simple *thuartpeatrick* (l. 10). First there is '*Tu es
Petrus*, thou art Peter, and upon this rock (Latin *petrus*) will I
build my church', the words of Christ to the disciple Simon
Peter, on which rests the Roman Catholic claim to supremacy
among the Christian churches. (Even Jesus was fond of a pun.)
The Irish Church was founded by Saint Patrick, and Ireland can
be characterristed by its peat ricks, stacks of turf for burning. So
far we can follow Joyce unaided. But he also refers in his notes
to 'the peatfire of faith' which responded to the windy words of
the apostle, 'avoice from afire' (afar) which 'bellowsed' (l. 9),
both cried out and blew up the flames.

In ll. 10–12 Joyce is referring to, among others, Jonathan
Swift, the Dean of St. Patrick's, Dublin, author of *Gulliver's
Travels*, whose life was enriched by the friendship of two
women with the same Christian name, Esther Vanhomrigh and
Esther Johnson, called by him Stella and Vanessa (*venissoon*, l. 10,
and *vanessy*, l. 12). Swift's christian name, Jonathan, is transmuted into *Nathandjoe*, two men in one, *twone*. Swift's love for

these young women is echoed in *sosie sesthers wroth*; Susannah in the Apocrypha was desired by the Elders; Esther by King Ahasuerus, and Ruth by the substantial mature farmer Boaz; and one theme of this book, as of mankind's history, is the love of father for daughter, of H. C. Earwicker for his daughter Isabel, or Issy.

A kidscad buttended a bland old isaac refers to Esau's deprivation of his birthright by his brother Jacob (another form of James); but it also alludes to that ever-present hero of Joyce's writings, the great Parnell who ousted the Irish nationalist leader Isaac Butt. And finally, *Jhem* and *Shen* are not only Noah's sons, Shem, Ham and Japhet, but also the perpetually quarrelling brothers Shem and Shaun, who can be *James* Joyce the creative artist, whose pen was wielded best in isolation (or exile) (*penisolate*, l. 6), and his more matter-of-fact aggressive public-spirited, politically-minded brother Stanislaus *John* Joyce, whose brotherly relationship never ran smoothly for long.

So far only the more obvious allusions in only fourteen lines have been looked at. To deal with the whole book at this length would take sixteen hundred times as long. Obviously this is not possible to an ordinary reader. Only people who are able to devote years of study to the book can hope to disentangle its verbal complexities. Joyce himself said it would keep the critics occupied for three hundred years, and there are many scholars who have made their living by working on *Finnegans Wake*: 15,000 words (a third of this book!) have been written on one sentence. Joyce's friends tried to turn him from his obsessional devotion to writing it. Not only Harriet Weaver, but also his staunch ally Ezra Pound, while formally wishing him every possible success, told him it was impossible to make anything of it—'I don't see what which has to do with where'—and that nothing short of a Divine Vision could be worth the expenditure of patience and ingenuity it demanded. Joyce went so far as to admit to Harriet Weaver, who wrote to state flatly that she did not much care for the output of his 'Wholesale Safety Pun Factory', that Pound might well be right, but he could not go back. In 1926, when these exchanges took place, a dozen years of work and worry still lay ahead before the book was to be finished. Joyce persevered with the obsessive devotion of genius—or madness.

Had Joyce not been living in Paris during the exciting years of the Dadaists and the Surrealists, it is possible that he might have been persuaded by the saner English or American intellectual climate to modify his extravagances or to give up the book altogether; in fact, he did at one time consider handing it over to someone else (James Stephens, the Irish poet) to finish. But he received encouragement from Eugene and Maria Jolas, a French-American couple who founded the new review, *transition*, on *avant-garde* lines (visible in the typography of the title, with its small *t*). Jolas had written a literary-revolutionary manifesto, liberally sprinkled with quotations from the archetypal rebel William Blake. In it he uttered such war-cries as 'Pure poetry is a lyrical absolute,' and 'the literary creator has the right to use words of his own fashioning' and to jettison ordinary syntax. This remarkable document ended: 'The writer expresses. He does not communicate. The plain reader be damned.'

The Jolas journal, *transition*, published several sections of the new book under the title 'Work in Progress' during the later twenties—Joyce mysteriously and childishly withheld the title *Finnegans Wake* until the eve of publication. Jolas and his circle made him the guru of the new movement. It is possibly this adulation that rendered him deaf to the sensible representations of those, like H. G. Wells, who spoke up for the common reader: 'I want language and statement as simple and clear as possible ... You have turned your back on common men ... Who the hell is this James Joyce who demands so many waking hours ... for a proper appreciation of his quirks and fancies and flashes of rendering?'

Joyce's answer would have been couched in terms that echoed the Jolas manifesto. 'Wideawake language, cut and dry grammar and go ahead plot', as he once called them, were useless to render sensible one great part of every human existence—the subconscious or semi-conscious dreaming part, the importance of which was recognised by Freud and later psychologists, and is nowadays taken for granted by all of us. Dreams are indeed essential to our mental health: if you are prevented from dreaming you go mad. The computer that is your brain needs sleep and dreams to assimilate the myriad impressions of waking life. *Finnegans Wake* is a dream; plot in the ordinary sense is less relevant to it even than it is to *Ulysses*, where a connected story can quite easily be followed. The language of everyday logical speech and discussion also lacks the flexibility necessary for accurately representing the shifting appearances and inconsequential phantasmagoria of the dream state. You can easily find out how inadequate language is by writing down one of your own dreams. We have seen Joyce's earlier attempts to put on paper the drunken consciousness of Stephen (in the 'Circe' chapter, XV, of *Ulysses*), the drowsy mind of Bloom (in the 'Nausicaa' chapter, XIII,) and the half-awake reverie of Molly ('Penelope,' Chapter XVIII). Here, with a little perseverance, common readers could follow him, and have found the journey rewarding. I doubt whether this is true of a good deal of *Finnegans Wake*.

At this very time, Virginia Woolf wrote her famous essay in *The Common Reader*, in which she castigates the 'materialistic' manner of Bennet, Wells and Galsworthy, the successful contemporary novelists. After reading one of their novels, she says, one is left with a feeling of sadness: with all their 'magnificent apparatus for catching life' it still escapes them. The writer should not feel constrained to provide a plot and an air of probability, for human consciousness is subject to 'an incessant shower of innumerable atoms'; life is thus 'a luminous halo, a semi-transparent envelope surrounding us from the beginning of consciousness to the end'. The writer's job is to record the atoms 'as they fall upon the mind', no matter how incoherent and disconnected the result will be. She goes on to praise Joyce's work for its attempt to 'reveal the flickerings of that innermost flame which flashes its message through the brain'; he had the courage to disregard adventitious elements such as probability or coherence, elements of narrative which are absent from the personal consciousness. In so doing he was removing those sign-posts which for generations had served to direct the reader when called upon to imagine the intangible.

Virginia Woolf's own work, of course, was another, less full-blooded, more ladylike attempt to do the same thing; her novels vary in the degree to which they reject plot, coherence and probability, but any reader of, say, *The Waves* will see the same process at work. [Those who do not know her work, and want to enlarge their experience in coping with a similar technique to Joyce's, should begin with *To the Lighthouse*: this would show how near she came to recording the atoms 'as they fall', yet what large areas of consciousness or subconsciousness she deliberately neglects. Unlike the full-bodied characters of Joyce, nobody in her books has an earthy thought; the sensations and feelings exposed are subtle and refined.]

One reply that Joyce constantly made to those who found *Finnegans Wake* impossible to proceed with was that they should read it as music, just enjoying the sound. As Jolas said, Pure poetry is a lyrical absolute, and to expect the new language to make what is normally regarded as sense is to ask what Mozart's Symphony No. 40 in G minor 'means'. It appears to record an almost neurotic frenzy of discontent and frustration; but it cannot be put into ordinary words; and any images it conjures up to one listener will be entirely individual to him. (There is an amusing attempt to capture in words Beethoven's Fifth Symphony in E. M. Forster's *Howards End*, Chapter V, but it is pretty trivial.)

So one piece of advice which may be offered to those who haven't the time or patience to struggle with the book that took Joyce sixteen years to write, is Joyce's own: try to read it as pure music. That it is pleasing to the ear was apparently enough justification for him, just as a picture or design is justified by being pleasing to the eye. To explore levels of meaning was unnecessary; the book was meant to entertain, not to instruct. '*In risu veritas*' (truth comes through laughter) was another defensive declaration that Joyce was fond of making.

For the great majority of students of James Joyce, *Finnegans*

Wake will always remain a largely unexplored continent. For those who wish to make the experiment of reading it musically probably the best place to start would be p. 196, the 'Anna Livia Plurabelle' chapter. This tremendous *tour de force* (though every chapter can lay claim to this epithet) contains the names of hundreds of rivers, reputedly over 500, but estimates differ, and I haven't made my own census. It purports on the surface to be the gossip of two old Dublin washerwomen who are laundering H. C. Earwicker's clothes in the waters of the Liffey, and enjoying the retailing of scandalous domestic details of the married life of HCE and ALP. As the twenty pages of beautifully witty writing proceed, the pace gradually slows, and finally the two gossips are transmogrified, one into a tree and the other into a stone, as twilight falls:

> Can't hear with the waters of. The chittering waters of. Flittering bats, fieldmice bawk talk. Ho! Are you not gone ahome? What Thom Malone? Can't hear with the bawk of bats, all thim liffeying waters of. Ho, talk save us! My foos won't moos. I feel as old as yonder elm. A tale told of Shaun or Shem? All Livia's daughter-sons. Dark hawks hear us. Night! Night! My ho head halls. I feel as heavy as yonder stone. Tell me of John or Shaun? Who were Shem and Shaun the living sons or daughters of? Night now! Tell me, tell me, tell me, elm. Night night! Telmetale of stem or stone. Beside the rivering waters of, hitherandthithering waters of. Night! FW. pp. 215–6

It took Joyce 1,200 hours, he claimed, to compose these twenty pages; and when you remember the day he spent on two sentences of *Ulysses* (see p. 56) this will not surprise you.

Joyce loved this section of the book more than any other, and asserted that he was prepared to stake everything on its success. There is a charming story of his saying that he hoped that some day some boy reading the book in Tibet or Somaliland would be pleased and excited by seeing in this chapter the name of his local river: another example of Joyce's universal imagination at work. Joyce's affection for 'Anna Livia Plurabelle' comes through very clearly in the famous gramophone record, now alas! unobtainable, of his own reading of the final pages.

It is beyond the scope of this short general introduction to James Joyce's Life and Works to embark on a detailed guide to *Finnegans Wake*. All that remains possible is to say briefly what the book is about.

The title derives from an Irish ballad about a Dublin brick-layer's labourer who fell from a building scaffold and broke his skull; his body was laid out for the wake (that peculiar custom in which friends assemble to watch over the dead man, with the aid of food, tobacco and drink, until the funeral) at which the whiskey and Guinness flowed so freely that the friends fell to drunken quarrelling. In the course of the ructions, the corpse was accidentally spattered with whiskey, which revived him. He rose and called for more.

This simple comic song is a parable of rebirth, of the cyclic view of history which Joyce derived from Vico. The corpse is planted in the earth, and from it spring the crops—giving Joyce his significant pun *cropse*, which can be said to summarise his philosophy in one word.

The title is printed punningly: notice that it has no apostrophe to signify the possessive case. It is not just the *wake* (itself a punning word) of Finnegan, but an assertion that all Finnegans, all Irishmen, all mankind, return from death again and again: the *fin*ish begins *again*—Finnegans wake.

So the book celebrates the complete history of all mankind in all ages, as the first sentence implies (see p. 130).

Obviously, the whole of mankind cannot appear in the space of 625 pages. So, just as Molly Bloom in *Ulysses* represents Gea-Tellus, the eternal feminine principle, so the five central characters of this book represent certain vital elements of every human family. They are the father, mother, daughter and twin sons. Father, the innkeeper, H. C. Earwicker (though he has other names), is every father, from Adam through Noah to the latest-married man. He is also the archetypal father-figure: God, the Pope, Cromwell (a much-hated figure in Catholic Ireland), the old Irish king Finn MacCool, King Arthur and any other famous Arthurs, whether the Duke of Wellington or the head of the Guinness brewing family. For this is the country of dreams, where identities shift and merge endlessly, as well as the real-life city of Dublin. Joyce constantly celebrated his own father, John Joyce, whether as Simon Dedalus or in his poems (see p. 48); and his love for the wayward spendthrift did not prevent him from sharp criticism of him. Joyce was also a loving father, who, as is stated on p. 17, sacrificed much of his and other people's happiness and comfort in the mistaken cause of saving his daughter Lucia from the psychiatrists and the mental hospital.

As Joyce loved Lucia, so every father loves his daughter, and HCE loves Issy or Isabel, the beautiful temptress. We all accept today the authority of Freud for regarding the family as an incestuously-consolidated unit. HCE is incestuously (but quite properly) in love with his daughter, who is of course to be responsible for the continuation of the race and the renewal of the family in another cycle of human history. Isabel is Isolde, or Iseult, but she is also every romantic heroine, every daughter of the original Eve, the temptress of Adam in the beginning of time.

Issy is one part of the woman-principle. The other and more important part is Anna Livia Plurabelle, ALP. She is at once all rivers, the Anna Liffey of Dublin as well as all the other 500 whose names are interwoven into her special chapter (FW pp. 196–216). She is the ever-forgiving wife of HCE, and she defends him against his gossiping denigrators. Hers are the final pages of the book, Book IV, pp. 619–28, in which she sings her death-song as she flows into the sea to begin again the cycle of life as a raincloud. 'Finn, again!' she calls, before she leads the reader back to the *riverrun* of the opening page. She is also the symbol of family solidarity and of the home and security; and we remember how Stephen Dedalus, in *A Portrait of the Artist as a Young Man* as well as in *Ulysses*, is constantly thinking of his mother. We also remember Nora Joyce, the home-maker, who had so much to put up with while her wayward obsessed husband was writing his 'chop-suey' of a book, as she called *Finnegans Wake*.

The two sons, best known as Shem and Shaun (Irish for James

and John), introduce another philosophical theme into Joyce's scheme: the theory of the identity of opposites. This attempts to explain the close connection, indeed the identity, of say laughter and tears, or love and hate—we commonly speak today of a love-hate relationship. Joyce adopted this theory from the 16th century Italian philosopher Bruno of Nola, whose name Joyce developed—transmuted in the dream—to that of Browne and Nolan, a Dublin firm of booksellers with whom he had had dealings. (Shem and Shaun are also at times confused with Browne and Nolan.) The twin boys, like all brothers from the days of Cain and Abel, quarrel and fight, only uniting to attack their father, HCE. Shem is James, the artist, the isolated romantic exile, Shem the Penman, or Punman, whereas Shaun is the active philistine man of affairs. It is tempting to equate these two with James and Stanislaus John Joyce, who were more or less estranged throughout their later life, as Stanislaus's title for his account of their early years, *My Brother's Keeper*, tends to show. (These are the words that Cain tried to hide behind when he had slain his brother Abel.) We know how barefacedly James relied on Stanislaus in their early years in Trieste, when James would squander his money on drink while Stanislaus's salary supported his brother's family (see p. 13). But Shem is also Cain, the one who shuns the company of ordinary men.

These then are the elements of the family. They can hardly be called characters in the accepted sense, since—as has been pointed out—there is no plot, and indeed no coherence at all. Their names appear again and again in changed and ever-changing forms; they also change roles, which increases the confusion but serves to emphasise Joyce's point, that somebody is everybody, and that HCE Haveth Childers Everywhere.

It is therefore unprofitable in this short chapter to attempt to come to terms with what little plot or story-line there is. But a glance at the shape of the book may serve to illuminate Joyce's purpose, just as *Ulysses* is made more intelligible by studying the complete schemes that Joyce gave to Linati and Stuart Gilbert.

Vico discerned four ages in each complete cycle of history, the Theocratic or Divine, the Aristocratic or Heroic, the

Democratic or Human, and finally the Ricorso or Return to the beginning. So *Finnegans Wake* is planned in cycles of four parts. Book I, pp. 3–216, has eight sections (two sets of four); Book II, pp. 219–399, has four sections; Book III, pp. 403–590, again has four; and then follows Book IV, a general return to the beginning, in only one section of thirty-six pages. Thus the four Books represent in turn the Divine Age, the Heroic Age, the Human Age, and the Return or Renewal.

It is generally considered that Books I and IV are the easiest to come at, generally speaking, and the most rewarding. Books II and III are positively boring in places; the third long section of Book III (pp. 474–554) is all about Yawn, a mutation from Shaun via the equally boring Jaun of section two (pp. 429–73). Here there is little beauty of sound and a good deal of nastiness and confusion, offering little reward—at least I myself have derived little pleasure from it.

Still, there the book stands, either a monumental folly or a sublime masterpiece that is too far in advance of public taste even thirty-five years after its publication. The best short defence of it is Richard Ellmann's, on pp. 729–30 of his life of Joyce (O.U.P.). Joyce's 'monster' had to be written, and Joyce was compelled to write it. His exploration of the sleeping, dreaming mind, in which 'all human activities begin to fuse into all other human activities', past, present and future, is a truly entertaining and revelatory feat. We know more about ourselves even if we can read only parts of it with a veiled understanding.

On the other hand. S. L. Goldberg, in his short book (see the Reading List, p. 146), has little but condemnation for it. Words are only symbols, and man is only what he says he is; therefore the attempt to encapsulate the essence of mankind in words is philosophically an impossible task and a self-defeating exercise.

The conflict between Life and Art that obsessed Yeats also bothered Joyce. But if Art could present Life, whole and real, warts and all, it would *become* Life. It would cease to be a way of distancing and taming the chaos of life, as a Mozart tune tames and orders the elements of wild bird-song; it would be a surrogate for life, in the pursuit of which life would cease to be lived. No one can spend his whole life absorbed in an artefact. Shem the Punman has created a divertissement, not an apocalypse.

For the ordinary man, then, *Finnegans Wake* will always remain too formidable an undertaking. Joyce died before he could inspire another Stuart Gilbert to do for this book what had been done for *Ulysses*.

Nevertheless for those intrepid readers who want to read the whole book in an intelligent, meaningful way there are several guides on the market which offer varying degrees of help. I have found extremely helpful one of the earliest: William York Tindall's *A Reader's Guide to James Joyce*, which since 1959 has added greatly to my pleasure in this difficult author. Sixty pages of this guide are devoted to *Finnegans Wake*, a meagre enough ration of space, but I would strongly recommend any beginner to look at them. Anthony Burgess has a considerable reputation as an interpreter of Joyce, and his *Here Comes Everybody* is more recent and perhaps more detailed; but it is often nearly as involved in its brilliant allusiveness as the original text it sets out to illuminate.

Anthony Burgess has also produced a *Shorter Finnegans Wake* as long ago as 1939. This reduces the formidable 623 pages to a more manageable 250, by selecting some of the best passages and connecting them with short narrative or explanatory links. A beginner would find it useful, after sampling 'Anna Livia Plurabelle' just to get the hang of things, to proceed to the *Shorter Finnegans Wake*.

An indispensable aid to further reading is Adaline Glasheen's *A Census of Finnegans Wake*, which dates from 1956, and is a concordance of most of the proper names in the book. Here you can trace some of the transmogrifications of the main 'characters': Cain and Abel, for instance, are listed either singly or together some thirty times, with page and line references, in such guises as *Cainandabler*, *cainozoic*, or—more remotely—*beam and cable*. Adaline Glasheen's brief synopsis of the story is also a useful stepping-off point.

There is also *A Skeleton Key to Finnegans Wake* by Joseph

Campbell and Henry Morton Robinson. This is useful but not as illuminating as its title promises. It is, however, now out of print.

Finally, for those interested in the language of *Finnegans Wake* there is a most balanced and enlightening chapter in John Gross's recent short essay in the Fontana Modern Masters Series. And for the reader who wants to come to terms with Joyce's whole method and design, A. Walton Litz's *The Art of James Joyce* is a fascinating exploration of Joyce's drafts and revisions, particularly in *Finnegans Wake*.

A Note on Parnell

Parnell: The Uncrowned King of Ireland. His name crops up frequently in all Joyce's prose works, and it is necessary to know more about him for a complete understanding of many passages.

A dozen years before James Joyce was born, an Irish Home Government Association was formed by Isaac Butt, with the declared aim of establishing a Parliament in Dublin, under the Queen and the Irish peers, with the object of making Ireland responsible for her own internal affairs. In 1875 Parnell, aged only twenty-nine, was elected to Westminster and by 1880 had risen to the leadership of the Irish Party in the Commons and of the Irish National Land League, founded by Michael Davitt, in the country. Though of typical Anglo-Irish land-owning stock—he was a useful cricketer and had spent some time at Cambridge University—Parnell campaigned against the stranglehold maintained by the absentee landlords over the rebellious and starving peasantry. Home Rule thus became integrated with Land Reform and formed an explosive compound.

Gladstone, the Liberal leader and Prime Minister, was not unsympathetic to the Home Rulers, though he took strong measures to put down the violence their cause generated. He imprisoned the leaders of the Land League; Parnell was actually in gaol when Joyce was born. As might have been expected, this repressive act served merely to inflame the populace and make heroes and martyrs of the victims. On Parnell's release, Gladstone worked with him to foster the Home Rule Bill, and though it failed to become law at the first attempt in 1886, the idea was gathering support, and all seemed set for a great Parnell triumph.

Then came the famous divorce case, in which Captain O'Shea cited Parnell as co-respondent with his wife Kitty: there was no defence, and after the decree nisi Parnell and Kitty were married. Today this would hardly have wrecked a politician's career; but all the moral forces of late Victorian Britain were ranged against the guilty pair. Gladstone, that embodiment of the non-conformist conscience, publicly withdrew his support; the Irish Party deposed Parnell from the leadership; and the Catholic Church in Ireland denounced him. He died soon after at the age of forty-five. Joyce was nine years old at the time, and in *A Portrait of the Artist as a Young Man* he reveals the impression made on him by talk of Parnell's astonishing funeral, when 150,000 mourners joined the procession to Glasnevin Cemetery (see p. 27 of *A Portrait*, though of course this describes a reverie in the boy's mind rather than an event). The devastating effect on ordinary folk of the Parnell tragedy is poignantly shown in 'Ivy Day in the Committee Room', a *Dubliners* story.

Parnell was useful to Joyce as a symbol of the nationalist aspirations of Ireland; he is also a stick to beat the Church with (Dante quarrels with Simon Dedalus and Mr. Casey over the Church's 'betrayal', *A Portrait*, pp. 31–40); and Kitty O'Shea becomes Issy the temptress in many references in *Finnegans Wake*. The Parnell story often occurs in references to cuckoldry and usurpers in *Ulysses*; Kitty O'Shea is connected in Bloom's mind with Molly, in for example pp. 569–76. Bloom also remembers how he picked up Parnell's hat and was thanked for returning it—unlike John Henry Menton (*Ulysses* p. 116); and Parnell's brother is pointed out as a sort of tourist attraction on p. 247.

Reading List

TEXTS

Chamber Music, 1907, Cape 1927 (1972)
Dubliners, 1914, Penguin 1956 (1968)
A Portrait of the Artist as a Young Man, 1916, Cape 1924, Penguin 1960 (1969)
Exiles, 1918, Cape 1921, NEL Signet Modern Classics 1968
Ulysses, Paris 1922, Bodley Head 1936, 1960, Penguin 1969 (1972)
Pomes Penyeach, Paris 1927, Faber 1966 (1971)
Finnegans Wake, Faber 1939 (1971)
Stephen Hero, ed. T. Spencer, 1944, Cape 1969
The Critical Writings of James Joyce, eds. Ellsworth Mason and Richard Ellmann, Faber 1959
Letters of James Joyce, vol. 1, ed. Stuart Gilbert, Faber 1957; vols. 2–3, ed. Richard Ellmann, Faber 1966

BIOGRAPHY

Richard Ellmann: *James Joyce*, O.U.P. 1959 (1965)
Stanislaus J. Joyce: *My Brother's Keeper*, Faber 1958
Frank Budgen: *James Joyce and the Making of Ulysses*, 1934, O.U.P. 1972

CRITICISM

Anthony Burgess: *Here Comes Everybody*, Faber 1965 (1969)
Samuel L. Goldberg: *Joyce*, Oliver & Boyd 1962 (1969)

Harry Levin: *James Joyce, a Critical Introduction*, Faber 1944, 1960 (1971)

A. Walton Litz: *The Art of James Joyce*, O.U.P. 1964

William York Tindall: *A Reader's Guide to James Joyce*, Thames & Hudson 1959 (1970)

Adaline Glasheen: *A Census of Finnegans Wake*, Faber 1957

John Gross: *Joyce*, Fontana/Collins 1971

Joseph Campbell and Henry Morton Robinson: *A Skeleton Key to Finnegans Wake*, Faber 1947

Michael Mason: *James Joyce, 'Ulysses'*, Arnold 1972

Richard Ellmann: *Ulysses on the Liffey*, Faber 1972

Stuart Gilbert: *James Joyce's Ulysses*, 1930, Faber 1952

Index